DECORATIVE
CROSS STITCH

DECORATIVE CROSS STITCH

Over 40 delightful designs for decorating items in your home

Maria Diaz

NEW HOLLAND

First published in 2003 by
New Holland Publishers (UK) Ltd
London · Cape Town · Sydney · Auckland

Garfield House, 86–88 Edgware Road
London W2 2EA
United Kingdom
www.newhollandpublishers.com

80 McKenzie Street
Cape Town 8001
South Africa

Level 1, Unit 4, 14 Aquatic Drive
Frenchs Forest, NSW 2086
Australia

218 Lake Road
Northcote, Auckland
New Zealand

ISBN 0-73943-477-2

Senior Editor: **Clare Sayer**
Production: **Hazel Kirkman**
Design: **Lisa Tai**
Photographer: **Shona Wood**
Illustrators: **Stephen Dew** and **Kate Simunek**
Editorial Direction: **Rosemary Wilkinson**

10 9 8 7 6 5 4 3 2 1

Reproduction by Modern Age Repro, Hong Kong
Printed and bound by Times Offset (M) Sdn Bhd, Malaysia

Special thanks to the following for stitching the finished projects:
Jane Chamberlain, Michaela Learner, Angela Ottewell,
Christine Thompson.

Contents

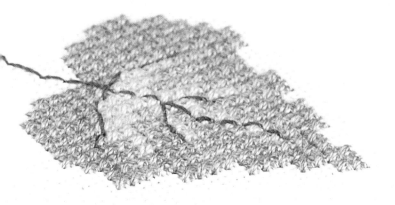

Introduction

Cross stitch first appeared in the sixteenth century and was traditionally used in samplers. Although samplers are now a design practice in their own right, they were first used as a reference for stitches and patterns and as a means for young embroiderers to practice their skills.

Once you have mastered the basic stitch, working with cross stitch is a wonderful way to create pictures. From really simple silhouettes to intricate flower studies, the technique is the same. Once you can read a pattern, you will be able to tackle the most elaborate designs with confidence. In this book, I have included a wide range of motifs to appeal to all tastes and skill levels, illustrating how versatile cross stitch can be.

Coming from a fine art background, I like to challenge the way cross stitch is perceived. As well as creating pictures, it is fun to come up with different ways in which to exhibit your stitching because if you become a fanatic, as many do, you will soon run out of wall space. From picnic baskets to address books, I enjoy adding little personal touches with cross stitch. Within this book, I have tried to show how easy it is to use your embroidery in more imaginative ways around the home. It doesn't have to be all napkins and antimacassars, you know.

Materials and techniques

Cross stitch is a simple stitch usually worked on evenweave linens or Aida (a specialty blockweave). The stitch itself is formed by two diagonal stitches, one lying diagonally over the other to create a cross. The stitches can be worked individually or "row by row," working a row of diagonal stitches (or half cross stitch) in one direction and then stitching back over them in the opposite direction to form the crosses. The following pages will provide you with all the information you need on materials, techniques, and caring for your finished items. All the materials and equipment used in this book can be easily obtained from good needlework or craft stores (see page 111 for more details).

FABRICS

Cross stitch is generally worked on evenweave fabrics such as Aida, hardanger, specialty evenweaves, and linens. Evenweave means that the same number of threads are counted in both directions over 1 in. (2.5 cm.) . It is sometimes referred to as 14-, 18-, or 28-count. Aida is a specially designed fabric where the fabric threads are set into blocks, giving a gridlike appearance and creating definite holes. Hardanger has its threads woven in pairs, again making it easy to see the holes. The specialty evenweaves and linens are loosely woven so you can count the threads and slip your needle through with ease.

When working on evenweave linen, it is usual to stitch over two of the fabric threads, which will essentially halve the fabric count, so a 28-count linen will give you only 14 stitches to the inch. It is important to remember this when working out design sizes.

Fabric counts are usually calculated in inches. To work out the finished size of a pattern, simply divide the number of stitches by the fabric count and that will give you a pretty accurate design size in inches. For example, a motif that is 40 stitches square and worked on a 14-count fabric, will measure about 3 in. (7.5 cm.) square, but on an 18-count it will be only 2¼ in. (6 cm.).

FLOSS

Stranded cotton is probably the most widely used embroidery floss on the market and comes as a 6-stranded length. You have to separate the strands one by one and then lay them back together in the quantities required. The number of strands required will vary depending on the fabric count; the chart below can be used as a guide.

Fabric count	Needle size	No. of stranded cotton strands
8-count	22	6—cross stitch 2—backstitch
11-count	24	3—cross stitch 1—backstitch
14-count, 16-count	26	2—cross stitch 1—backstitch
18-count 22-count	26	1—cross stitch 1—backstitch

NEEDLES

Tapestry needles are most often used when working cross stitch as they have a large eye and blunt end, which are easily pushed through the natural holes of the fabric.

Chenille needles have a larger eye than embroidery needles and are the best ones to use when working with waste canvas.

You need to choose an appropriate size of needle, which will depend on the floss and fabric used; the chart opposite can be used as a guide.

Above: Cross stitch fabrics, stranded cottons, and needles are the only essential materials you need to do a cross stitch project, but the following items are also useful: embroidery scissors, dressmaking scissors, tape measure, basting thread, sewing thread, and pins, as well as embroidery hoops to keep the fabric taut while you work.

CHARTS

Cross stitch charts are easy to read, each square on the pattern representing one stitch. Quarter and three-quarter stitches are used only when a square is divided diagonally in half and has a tiny symbol in one or both sections. Backstitch is usually shown as a bold line.

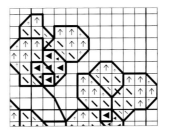

Left: This chart is a detail of the smaller chart on page 62. In this case, the small arrow symbol taking up just half of one square represents a quarter stitch. The bold lines indicate where backstitch is required.

EMBROIDERY HOOPS AND FRAMES

Embroidery hoops and frames come in a range of sizes from tiny 3 in. (8 cm.) hoops for small motifs to large freestanding frames for heirloom projects. It is always best wherever possible to use a frame or hoop. They are designed to keep the fabric taut while stitching, which in turn helps to regulate the tension of your sewing and keep the stitches even. Do not stretch the fabric too tightly in the hoop, and remove the hoop when not stitching, to prevent permanent distortions to your stitches or fabric.

ADDITIONAL EQUIPMENT

There are a few other essentials you will need to have to hand. Dressmaking scissors for cutting your fabric, embroidery scissors for trimming floss, and contrasting basting thread to indicate center marks and guide lines. For making up your projects you will need a basic sewing kit (tape measure, pins, embroidery floss, needles, scissors), sewing machine, and additional fabrics and trimmings, which will be individually listed for each project.

AFTER CARE

When you have finished a project, it can look a little creased and grubby, so knowing how to clean the materials used is important. Most floss on the market today is colorfast, but do read the manufacturer's directions before washing anything. If you are choosing a floss for an item which will require regular cleaning, ensure that it is colorfast, or the time you spend sewing could be longer than the life of that item!

Depending on the fabric used, virtually all your work can be hand washed carefully in warm water using a mild detergent. It is even possible to use your washing machine on a delicate cycle as long as the fabric edges are finished properly and all stray strands are firmly secured.

Once washed, it is best to press the stitching while still damp, as ironing will restore the stiffness lost during sewing. Place the stitched piece face down onto a towel to prevent the stitches being flattened. Using a cool iron, press carefully.

GETTING STARTED

When working a counted cross stitch design, it is always best (unless otherwise directed) to start stitching from the center of the pattern and work outward. This will ensure the motif's correct position on the fabric. Cross stitch patterns usually have the centers indicated. The easiest way to find the fabric center is as follows: fold the fabric in half vertically and horizontally and then press firmly on the folds to create definite creases. When the fabric is laid out flat again, it will be divided into fourths. Using a contrasting color to the fabric, work a line of basting along each crease—where they cross is the center of the fabric piece.

A good tip is to overestimate your fabric size, leaving yourself about an extra 1 in. (2 cm.) all the way round. This enables you to secure your edges and leaves you room for mistakes (such as not starting right in the center or forgetting to allow room for wording around the design). It is also a good idea to secure the fabric edges to prevent fraying. This can be achieved by binding, oversewing, or zigzagging with a sewing machine.

STARTING AND FINISHING

Working from the front, push the needle through about 1½ in. (4 cm.) to one side, bringing it back through where you intend to begin. Start stitching the first line, making sure you catch in the floss at the back. Once it is secure, pull the loose end through. If this proves difficult, simply pull the end through to the back when you have finished stitching. Thread it through the needle and darn the end under a few stitches to secure. This is also the best way to finish off—it is important not to use knots because these create lumps and may eventually work loose or snag.

Individual cross stitch

Looking at the stitch as a square, bring the needle out in the bottom right corner and work a diagonal stitch to top left. Then bring the needle through in the bottom left and cross the first stitch with another diagonal stitch into the top right corner.

Cross stitch, row-by-row

Work a row of diagonal stitches from bottom right to top left. Then work a row of diagonal stitches in the opposite direction, crossing the first ones. I work this way as I am right-handed, so I do not drag my hand across the finished stitches. However it is not important which way you work as long as all the top diagonals face the same direction.

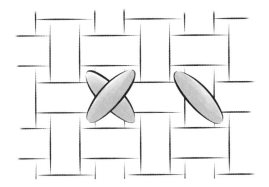

Individual cross stitch and half cross stitch

Cross stitch, row-by-row

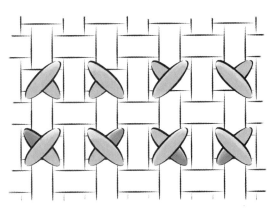

Quarter and three-quarter stitches

Back stitch

Half cross stitch

Half cross stitch is a single diagonal stitch, which is half a cross stitch. It can be worked from either bottom right to top left, or from bottom left to top right.

Quarter and three-quarter stitches

Quarter and three-quarter stitches fill in half the space of a full cross stitch on the chart. Stitch one diagonal (or half cross stitch) and then, instead of working the crossing stitch from corner to corner, pass it through the center of the stitch.

A quarter stitch is simply half of a diagonal (or half cross stitch), worked from corner to middle.

Back stitch

Work a single straight stitch, then bring the needle out one stitch length ahead and then back to link up the line. Backstitch can be worked in any direction and is used to outline designs and add detail.

French knots

French knots are great for adding texture and work well within cross stitch designs. Holding the floss taut, wrap it twice around the needle. Then, still holding the floss taut, insert the needle back into the fabric close to where it emerged and pull the floss through.

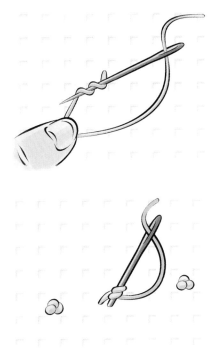

French knots

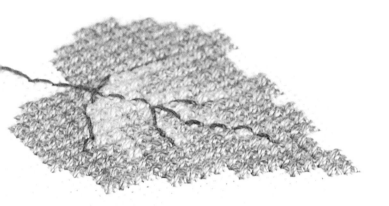

Fruit and Flower Motifs

We often look to nature and wonder at her beauty and elegance. Here we have a taste of how that charm can be portrayed in cross stitch. From simple daisy motifs dancing along a picnic cloth to intricate flower studies, this chapter has something for every skill level.

Summer fruits

Brighten up your kitchen with some luscious red fruits or label your preserve pots with specific motifs. These fruit motifs are simple but effective and can be stitched onto all manner of items—not just items for the home. These fun kitchen accessories are the perfect thing for the organic gardener.

SKILL LEVEL: 1

MEASUREMENTS

When worked on 14-count Aida with each cross stitch worked over one fabric block, the strawberry motif for the jelly pot cover measures 1½ x 1 in. (4 x 3 cm.). The strawberry and cherry motif (which is repeated along the band) measures 4 x 1 in.(10 x 3 cm.).

YOU WILL NEED
For the embroidery
- 8 in. (20 cm.) 14-count white Aida
- 2 in. (5 cm.) Aida band (dish towel width)
- Tapestry needle, size 26
- Embroidery hoop
- Scissors
- Contrasting basting thread
- Soft pencil
- DMC stranded cottons as listed

To make up the projects
- Basic sewing kit
- Sewing machine
- Matching sewing thread
- Bias binding
- Plain dish towel

Color		Shade	No. of skeins
■	red	350	1
■	peach	351	1
■	bright green	702	1
□	lime green	704	1
■	brown	779	1
■	blue	798	1
■	dark red	817	1
□	light green	913	1
□	pale mint	955	1
□	white	blanc	1

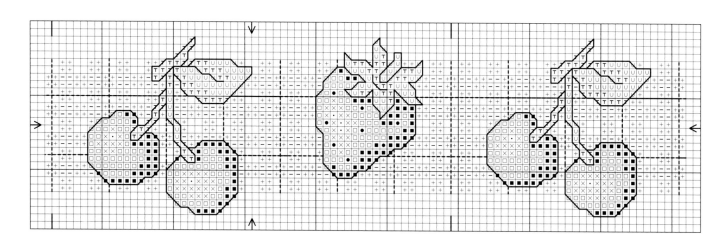

Symbol	Color	Backstitch	Shade
▢	red		350
⊠	peach		351
T	bright green		702
U	lime green		704
	brown	◥	779
	blue	◢	798
▣	dark red		817
⊟	light green		913
⊞	pale mint		955
⊡	white		blanc

Above: A strawberry motif on a jelly pot cover.

Right: Repeat the design along the Aida band to fit your item.

DISH TOWEL BAND

1 To calculate the amount of Aida band required, measure the width of your dish towel and add 1 in. (2 cm.).

2 Fold the band in half and mark the center with basting. Then fold lengthwise to find the horizontal center and baste another short line. Where the lines cross, marks the center and starting point.

3 Using two strands of cotton for cross stitch and one for backstitch, work the design shown on the chart opposite.

4 Repeat the design along the band, leaving a gap of 1½ in. (4 cm.) at either end. [Repeat marks are indicated as short black lines on the chart.]

5 Remove the basting and press with a cool iron. Position the Aida band on the dish towel, then pin and baste in place. Machine or slip stitch in place, remembering to turn under the end of the band to keep it neat.

JELLY POT COVER

1 Cut a 8-in. (20-cm.) square of 14-count white Aida and bind the edges using colored bias binding.

2 Mark the center of the fabric with basting. With a soft pencil , indicate on the chart the center of a single fruit.

3 Using two strands of cotton for cross stitch and one for backstitch, stitch the motif from the center out.

4 When complete, remove the basting and press with a cool iron.

Art Deco rose sewing set

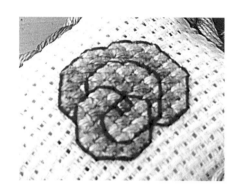

These stylish Art Deco Rose accessories would be a delightful addition to any needlework enthusiast's sewing box. In clear yet subtle shades, the simple symmetry reflects the chic elegance of the Deco era. A pretty pincushion, needle case, and scissor fob mean that you will always have your essential sewing kit to hand.

SKILL LEVEL: 1

MEASUREMENTS
Worked on 14-count Aida and with each cross stitch worked over one fabric block, the scissor fob motif measures 1 x 1 in. (2 x 2 cm.), the needle case motif measures 2½ x 1½ in. (6 x 4 cm.) and the pincushion measures 4 x 4 in. (9 x 9 cm.).

YOU WILL NEED
For the embroidery
- 5 in. (14 cm.) square, white 14-count Aida
- 6½ x 4 in. (17 x 11 cm.) white 14-count Aida
- 2½ in. (6 cm.) square, white 14-count Aida
- Tapestry needle, size 26
- Embroidery hoop
- Scissors
- Contrasting basting thread
- DMC stranded cottons as listed

To make up the projects
- Basic sewing kit
- Sewing machine
- Pinking shears
- Polyester stuffing
- 10 x 4 in. (25 x 11 cm.) piece of felt
- 10 in. (25 cm.) square backing fabric
- 3 ft. (1 m.) coordinating cord

	Color	Shade	No. of skeins
	emerald green	562	1
	pale green	563	1
	burgundy	902	1
	dusky pink	3687	1
	light pink	3688	1

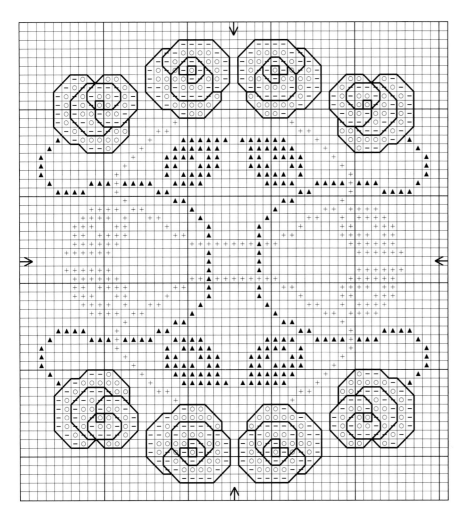

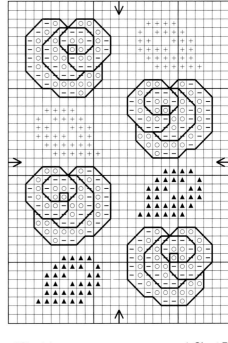

◁ Chart A   △ Chart B

Symbol	Color	Backstitch	Shade
▲	emerald green		562
+	pale green		563
	burgundy	◹	902
⊙	dusky pink		3687
⊟	light pink		3688

PINCUSHION

1 Mark the center of a 5 in. (14 cm.) square of Aida with basting.

2 Using two strands of stranded cotton for cross stitch and one for backstitch, work the pincushion design (chart A) from the center out over one fabric block.

3 When you have completed the stitching, remove the basting and gently press on the reverse with a cool iron.

4 Cut backing fabric into a 5 in. (14 cm.) square. Lay the backing fabric and stitched piece together, right sides facing, then pin and baste in place.

5 With a ½ in. (1 cm.) seam allowance, stitch together, leaving a 2½ in. (6 cm.) gap in one side to turn through.

6 Remove basting and turn right side out, gently pushing out the corners. Fill the cushion with polyester stuffing and slipstitch the gap shut.

7 Finally, using slipstitch again in a matching color, attach a coordinating cord around the edge, leaving a loop at one corner.

Left: A single rose motif adorns the scissor fob while the needle case has a pattern of roses and leaves.

SCISSOR FOB

1 Take a 2½ in. (6 cm.) square of Aida and mark the center with basting.

2 Using two strands for cross stitch and one for backstitch, stitch a single rose motif from the center out over one fabric block.

3 When you have completed the stitching, remove the basting and gently press.

Above: Choose a cord in a coordinating color to trim the pincushion.

4 Cut backing fabric to a 2½ in. (6 cm .) square and follow steps 4–6 for the pincushion above to make up the tiny cushion.

5 When the cushion is finished, stitch a cord all the way round with a 3 in. (7 cm.) long loop to one corner, so that it can be attached to your scissors.

NEEDLE CASE

1 Cut a 6½ x 4 in. (17 x 11 cm.) piece of Aida. Fold the fabric in half widthwise, marking out the center of the right half with basting. Stitch the needle case design (chart B) from the center of this half. Using two strands for cross stitch and one for backstitch, work over one fabric block. Remove basting and press.

2 Trim the Aida eight blocks from the design along the top, bottom, and right-hand side and 3½ in. (9 cm.) from the left of the design.

3 Fray the fabric on all four sides by carefully pulling out two blocks of threads.

4 Measure the finished size of the design and then, using pinking shears, cut a piece of felt ½ in. (1 cm.) larger all round. Again using pinking shears, cut another piece of felt half the size of the first.

5 With the stitching face down, place the largest piece of felt over the top, then position the smaller piece in the center on top of that.

6 Pin, then stitch all three layers together in one line down the center and fold in half to form a book.

Red poppies

Bring a touch of the fall harvest into your home with this stunning poppy picture and matching cushion. Modern and stylish, this rich red flower study is given a hint of rustic charm when stitched onto natural linen and made up into a bench cushion with chunky wooden buttons.

SKILL LEVEL: 2

MEASUREMENTS

Worked on 32-count linen with each cross stitch worked over three fabric threads, the picture motif measures 8½ x 4½ in. (21 x 12 cm.). With each stitch worked over two fabric threads, the cushion motif measures 5½ x 3 in. (14 x 8 cm.).

YOU WILL NEED

For the embroidery
- 16 x 12 in. (40 x 30 cm.) 32-count white Belfast linen
- 17¼ x 20½ in. (44 x 26 cm.) 32-count natural Belfast linen
- Tapestry needle, size 26
- Tapestry needle, size 24
- Embroidery hoop
- Scissors
- Contrasting basting thread
- DMC stranded cottons as listed

To make up the projects
- Basic sewing kit
- Sewing machine
- White sewing thread
- 4 x large wooden buttons
- 34¾ x 21¼ in. (88 x 54 cm.) white linen
- 23½ x 16 in. (60 x 40 cm.) cushion pad

Color	Shade	No. of skeins
burned rose	221	1
black	310	1
dark green	319	1
coral	350	1
peach	352	1
apple	471	1
red	817	1
grass green	989	1
pale green	3348	1
forest green	3363	1
green	3364	1
tangerine	3825	1

PICTURE

1 Fold the 16 x 12 in. (40 x 30 cm.) piece of white 32-count linen in half horizontally and vertically. With contrasting thread, stitch a line of basting along each crease. This marks the fabric center.

2 With a size 24 needle, begin stitching from the center out, using three strands for cross stitch and French knots and two for the backstitch. Work each stitch over three fabric threads.

3 When all the stitching has been completed, remove the basting and press.

4 Either frame the design yourself or take to a professional.

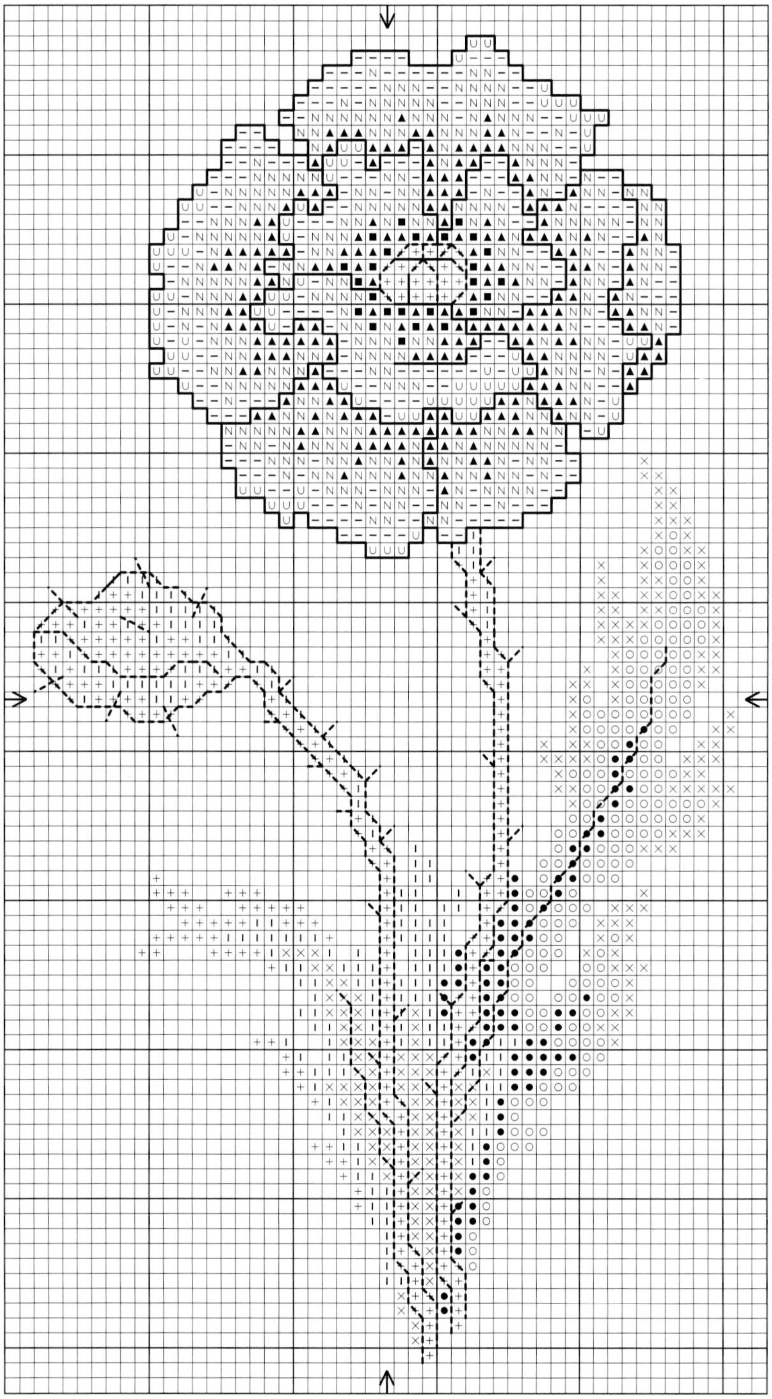

Symbol	Color	Backstitch	Shade
	burned rose		2211
	dark green		319
N	coral		350
–	peach		352
I	apple		471
▲	red		817
×	grass green		989
+	pale green		3348
●	forest green		3363
○	green		3364
U	tangerine		3825

Symbol	Color	French knot	Shade
	black		310

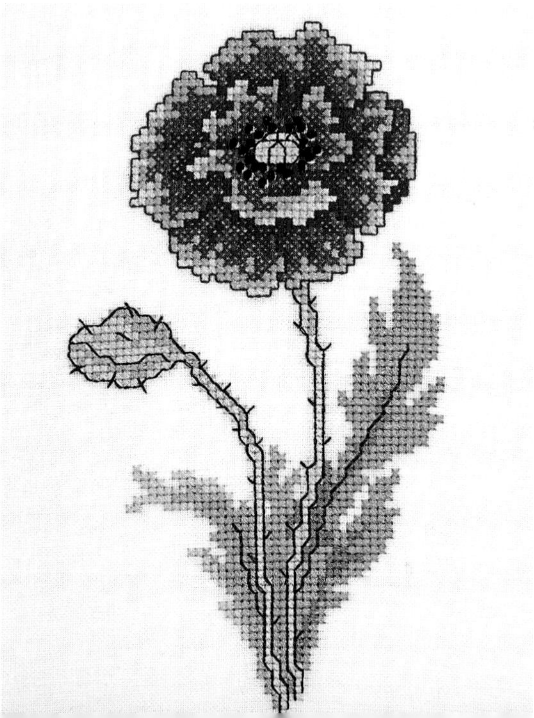

Right: Worked over three fabric threads, the poppy motif is larger.

CUSHION COVER

1 Cut your piece of natural linen in half so you have two 17¼ x 10¼ in. (44 x 26 cm.) pieces. Mark the center of one piece with basting.

2 With a size 26 needle, begin stitching, using two strands for cross stitch and French knots and one for the backstitch. Work each stitch over two fabric threads. When complete, remove the basting and press.

3 Cut your piece of white linen in half so that you have two 21¼ x 17¼ in. (54 x 44 cm.) pieces.

4 Lay the stitched piece and one white piece right sides together . Taking a 1¼ in. (3 cm.) seam allowance, stitch their right-hand edges together. Repeat with the other two pieces.

5 Zigzag or oversew the edges to prevent fraying and press the seams open.

6 Fold over 1½ in. (4 cm.), then 2¼ in. (6 cm.) at the opposite end to the natural linen on each piece (see diagram A). Pin and baste in place. These now make up the front and back of your cushion.

7 On the front cushion panel (the one with the stitching), stitch four buttonholes that are 3¼ in. (8 cm.) apart.

8 Place the two panels right sides together. Then, taking a 3 cm (1¼ in) seam allowance, stitch three sides together, leaving the end with the buttonholes open (see diagram B).

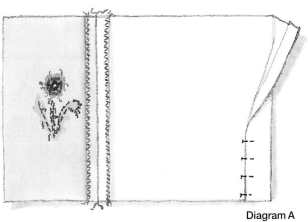

Diagram A

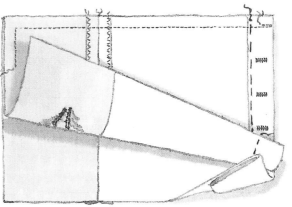

Diagram B

9 Remove all the basting, then zigzag or oversew the edges to prevent fraying. Turn right side out and press, then stitch the four buttons in place and put in your cushion pad.

Left: The cushion motif is smaller when stitched over two fabric threads.

Green leaves table linen

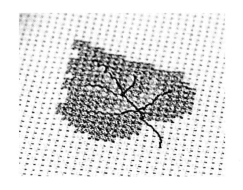

Bring a touch of the outdoors into your dining room with these wonderful fresh green leaves. They are the perfect motifs to add a hint of nature to your table linen. Scatter them across a tablecloth or use single motifs to bring a touch of style to napkins and accessories.

SKILL LEVEL: 2

MEASUREMENTS
Worked on the Bornholm tablecloth, the largest leaf motif measures 2 x 1¾ in. (5 x 4.5 cm.). The napkin motif measures 1½ x 1½ in. (3.5 x 3.5 cm.).

NOTE
Measurements and quantities given are for one tablecloth, two napkins, and two coasters.

YOU WILL NEED
For the embroidery
- E1310, Bornholm table cloth
- 24 x 24 in. (60 x 60 cm.) 28-count evenweave linen
- Tapestry needle, size 26
- Embroidery hoop
- Scissors
- Contrasting basting thread
- White sewing thread
- DMC stranded cottons as listed

To make up the projects
- Basic sewing kit
- Sewing machine
- Acrylic coaster

Color		Shade	No. of skeins
	dusky green	320	1
	light green	368	1
	pale mint	369	1
	apple green	471	1
	lime green	472	1
	bright green	989	2
	dark green	3362	1
	forest green	3363	1
	leaf green	3364	1

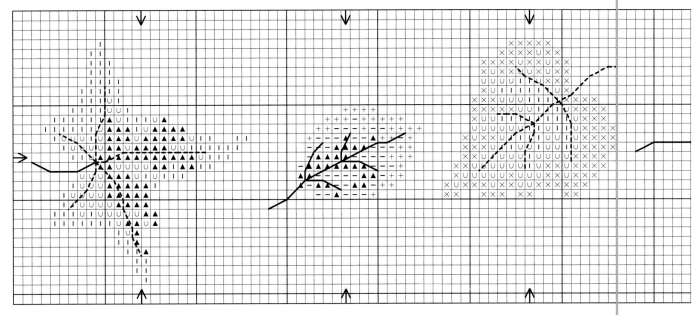

Symbol	Color	Backstitch	Shade
▲	dusky green		320
−	light green		368
+	pale mint		369
U	apple green		471
I	lime green	◩	472
×	bright green		989
■	dark green	◪	3362
●	forest green		3363
○	leaf green		3364

Above: Choose one of the leaves to stitch onto a napkin.

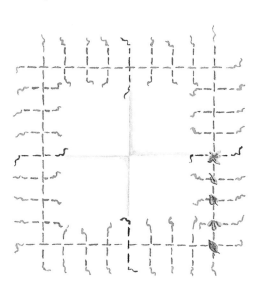

Left: The diagram shows where you should position the leaves along the edges of the tablecloth.

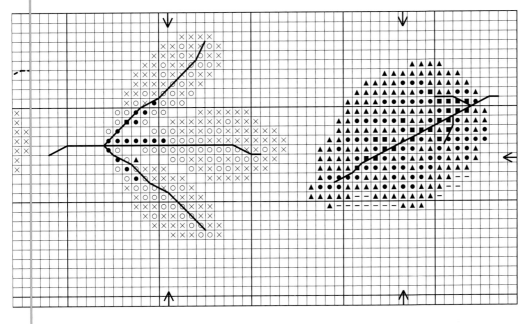

Below: The acrylic coaster keeps the motif in pristine condition.

TABLECLOTH

1 Stitch a line of basting 17 blocks in from the panel edge on all four sides. Fold the cloth in half vertically and horizontally and stitch a short line of basting down each crease crossing the basted square. This will mark the central point of each side.

2 Stitch three short lines either side of the center line at equal intervals between the central point and the basted corner (see diagram opposite). This will give you 32 intersections, marking the center of each leaf to be stitched.

3 Using two strands of cotton for cross stitch and one for backstitch, work each stitch over one fabric block. Start from the central point on one side and work the first leaf from the center out. Following the chart, stitch each leaf in sequence from left to right. Then stitch the leaves in reverse order to the left, omitting the last leaf.

4 Once you have completed the first side, turn the cloth 90° and stitch the next quarter. Continue like this until all four quarters are finished. Remove the basting and gently press with a cool iron.

NAPKIN

1 Hem a 12 in. (30 cm.) square of evenweave linen by folding over ⅜ in. (1 cm.), then ½ in. (1.5 cm.) and machine stitch in place.

2 Then, in one corner, baste two short lines running parallel with the edges about 4 in. (10 cm.) in from the hemmed edge. Using where they cross as the central mark, stitch a single leaf.

3 Using two strands of floss for cross stitch and one for backstitch, work each stitch over two fabric threads. Remove the basting and gently press with a cool iron.

COASTER

1 Cut a piece of evenweave linen 6 in. (15 cm.) square.

2 Mark the center and stitch a single leaf using two strands of cotton for cross stitch and one for backstitch. Work each stitch over two fabric threads.

3 When complete, back with Vilene and make up the coaster using the supplier's directions.

Daisy picnic basket

Why not add a hint of nostalgia to your summer day trips by dressing up an old basket to carry all your picnic treats in? These delicate white daisies look pretty, yet modern when stitched onto rich blue linen, making these the perfect accessories for a lazy summer picnic.

SKILL LEVEL: 2

MEASUREMENTS

Worked on 32-count linen with each cross stitch worked over two fabric threads, the tablecloth motif (which is repeated to make a border) measures 4 x 2½ in. (10 x 6 cm.). A single daisy motif measures 2 x 2 in. (5 x 5 cm.).

YOU WILL NEED

For the embroidery
- 24 in. (60 cm.) 32-count regal blue, Belfast linen
- Tapestry needle, size 26
- Embroidery hoop
- Scissors
- Contrasting basting thread
- Matching sewing thread
- DMC stranded cottons as listed

To make up the projects
- Basic sewing kit
- Sewing machine
- 6 ft. (1.8 m.) coordinating fabric
- 6½ ft. (2 m.) of 1¼-in. (3-cm.) wide coordinating ribbon
- 15½ ft. (40 cm.) medium weight batting
- Brown paper and pencil
- Basket

Color		Shade	No. of skeins
	light green	164	2
	light sand	676	1
	dark sand	729	1
	palest pink	819	1
	light pink	963	2
	grass green	988	1
	silver plum	3042	1
	white	blanc	2

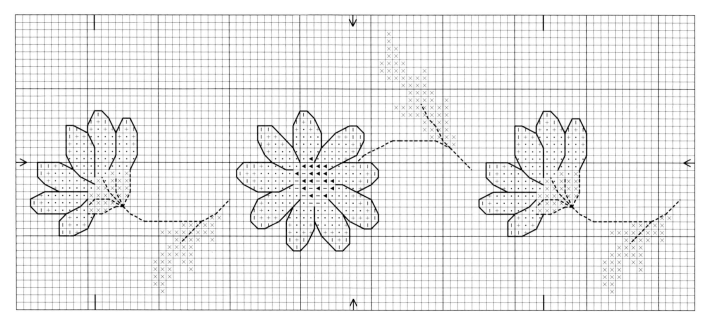

△ Chart A

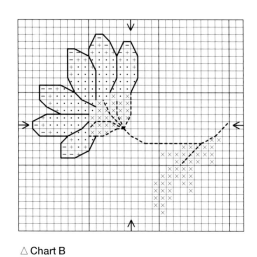

△ Chart B

Symbol	Color	Backstitch	Shade
⊠	light green		164
Ⅰ	light sand		676
▲	dark sand		729
＋	palest pink		819
－	light pink		963
	grass green	◨	988
	silver plum	◩	3042
⊡	white		blanc

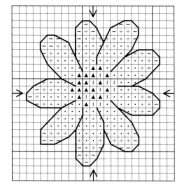

△ Chart C

Right: The daisy motif is repeated to fit the length of the tablecloth.

PICNIC CLOTH

1 Cut a strip of linen 8¼ in. (21 cm.) wide (fabric is supplied in 55 in./140 cm. widths) and mark the fabric center with basting.

2 Using two strands of stranded cotton for cross stitch and one for backstitch, work each stitch over two fabric threads. Start stitching from the center out (see chart A).

3 Using the repeat marks as a guide (indicated in bold lines on the chart), continue stitching the daisies along the whole length of the fabric. Finish with a complete flower at least 4 in. (10 cm.) from either end.

4 Once you have completed the stitching, remove the basting thread and press gently with a cool iron on the wrong side.

5 Taking a 1¼ in. (3 cm.) hem allowance and with the right sides facing, attach the embroidered piece down the length of a coordinating piece of fabric 55 x 47¼ in. (140 x 120 cm.) to form your picnic cloth.

6 Press open the seam and zigzag or overstitch the edges to prevent fraying. Finally, hem the whole cloth, turning over ¾ in. (2 cm.), then 1¼ in. (3 cm.).

PICNIC BASKET

1 Use the brown paper to make a pattern for the basket lid. Place the paper over the basket and notch out a space for the handles. Trim round the shape leaving about a 1¼ in. (3 cm.) overhang.

2 Using this pattern, cut a piece of linen, coordinating fabric and batting to shape.

3 Randomly stitch a selection of daisies across the linen, making sure the motifs are at least 4 in. (10 cm.) in from the edges (charts B and C). Once you have completed the stitching, press gently with a cool iron on the wrong side of the stitching.

Above: Single daisies are stitched randomly onto the basket cover.

4 Taking the piece of coordinating fabric, pin and then baste the ribbon all the way round the edge. Cut the remaining ribbon into four equal lengths and baste to either side of the handle area (see diagram A).

5 Lay the embroidered and coordinating fabric pieces together with the ribbon and the cross stitch on the inside. Place the batting on top and pin, then baste the three layers together (see diagram B).

6 Taking a ½ in. (1.5 cm.) seam allowance, stitch the layers together, leaving a 8 in. (20 cm.) gap to turn through.

7 When you have stitched all three layers securely together, turn right side out and slipstitch the gap shut.

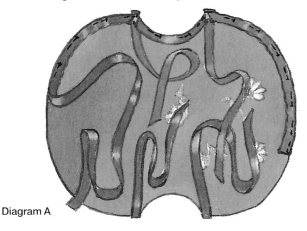

Diagram A

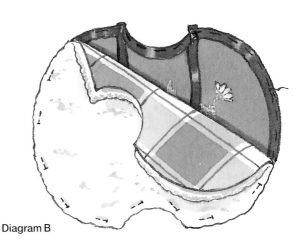

Diagram B

Camellia bed linen

This pretty pink camellia design is the perfect motif for beautiful bed linen. Depending on what size it is used at, the motif has different effects: 10-count waste canvas is used to make a bold statement on the pillowcase, but the same motif appears more delicate and precious when stitched onto linen.

SKILL LEVEL: 3

MEASUREMENTS

Worked on 10-count waste canvas, the pillow motif measures 5½ x 5½ in. (14 x 14 cm.). With each cross stitch worked over one fabric block, the sheet motif measures 3 x 3 in. (8 x 8 cm.). Worked on 32-count linen with each cross stitch worked over two fabric threads, the trinket box motif measures 3 x 3 in. (8 x 8 cm.).

NOTE

Measurements and quantities given are for a single sheet. Double the number of motifs and thread quantities for a double or king-size sheet.

YOU WILL NEED
For the embroidery

- 7 in. (18 cm.) square of 10-count waste canvas
- 5½ in. (14 cm.) white Aida band (sheet width)
- 7 x 7 in. (18 x 18 cm.) white 32-count linen
- Tapestry needle, size 26
- Chenille needle, size 24
- Embroidery hoop
- Scissors
- Contrasting basting thread
- DMC stranded cottons as listed

To make up the projects
- Basic sewing kit
- Sewing machine
- White sewing thread
- Tweezers
- Trinket box

Color		Shade	No. of skeins
	darkest green	500	1
	mid sand	676	1
	light sand	677	1
	dark sand	729	1
	palest pink	819	2
	soft pink	963	2
	forest green	987	1
	fresh green	988	2
	light green	989	1
	warm pink	3716	2
	dark terracotta	3721	1
	white	blanc	2

Symbol	Color	Backstitch	Shade
	darkest green		500
○	mid sand		676
−	light sand		677
Z	dark sand		729
+	palest pink		819
I	soft pink		963
▲	forest green		987
□	fresh green		988
✕	light green		989
●	warm pink		3716
	dark terracotta		3721
·	white		blanc

SHEET BAND

1 To calculate the amount of Aida band required, measure the width of your sheet and add 2 in. (5 cm.).

2 Fold the band in half and mark the center with a line of basting. Stitch two further lines at 10 in. (25 cm.) intervals to either side. Then fold lengthwise to find the horizontal center and baste a series of short lines crossing the first ones. Where the lines cross, marks the center and starting point of each motif.

3 Using two lengths of stranded cotton for cross stitch and one for backstitch, work each stitch over one fabric block.

4 When you have completed all the motifs, remove the basting. Using a cool iron, press the band gently from the wrong side.

5 Pin and baste the Aida band about 3 in. (8 cm.) from the top of the sheet, with the design upside down so that when the sheet is turned over it will read the right way.

6 Either machine or slip stitch in place, remembering to turn in the untidy end of the band to keep it neat.

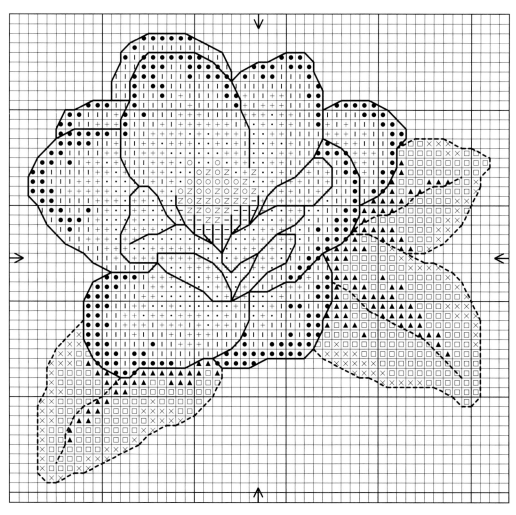

Left: The motifs are stitched onto Aida band and then attached to a sheet.

PILLOW CASES

1 Cut a 7 in. (18 cm.) square of waste canvas and mark the center with basting.

2 Position the canvas on the pillowcase where you want your camellia motif to be and baste into place, remembering to stitch through only one layer.

3 With an embroidery hoop to keep the canvas and pillowcase layer taut, stitch the motif, using the chenille needle. Use four strands for cross stitch and two for backstitch.

4 When the motif has been completed, remove all the basting and damp down the waste canvas. Pull the canvas threads out one at a time using tweezers, then gently press using a cool iron.

TRINKET BOX

1 Cut a 7 in. (18 cm.) square of linen and mark the center.

2 Using two lengths of stranded cotton for cross stitch and one for backstitch, work each stitch over two fabric threads.

3 Remove the basting and press. Make up the trinket box lid using the supplier's directions.

Left: A matching trinket box completes the bedroom set.

Picture Motifs

The reflective qualities of many of the flosses used can give pictures and motifs a wonderful sense of texture and depth by manipulating the shades and colors, as one would with painting or drawing. The projects illustrate the different styles you can achieve using the same stitch.

Seashell bathroom

These pretty pink shells are the perfect thing to add some seashore charm to your bathroom. Stitch up a few shells and then frame them to make a sweet little picture or take just one shell motif and repeat it across a towel for a guest bathroom.

SKILL LEVEL: 1

MEASUREMENTS
The towel motif measures 2½ x 1½ in. (6.5 x 3.5 cm.). Worked on 18-count Aida with each cross stitch worked over one fabric block, the largest picture motif measures 2 x 1½ in. (5 x 3.5 cm.).

YOU WILL NEED
For the embroidery
- 7 x 5½ in. (18 x 14 cm.) white 18-count Aida
- Guest towel with 3 in. (8 cm.) Aida panel
- Tapestry needle, size 26
- Embroidery hoop
- Scissors
- Contrasting basting thread
- DMC stranded cottons as listed

To make up the projects
- A frame of your choice

Color		Shade	No. of skeins
☐	palest pink	819	1
☐	baby pink	963	1
◼	dark pink	3350	1
◼	raspberry	3685	1
◼	rose pink	3731	1
◼	soft rose	3733	1
☐	white	blanc	1

Symbol	Color	Backstitch	Shade
I	palest pink		819
X	baby pink		963
□	dark pink		3350
■	raspberry	◨	3685
−	rose pink		3731
○	soft rose		3733
+	white		blanc

▷ Chart A

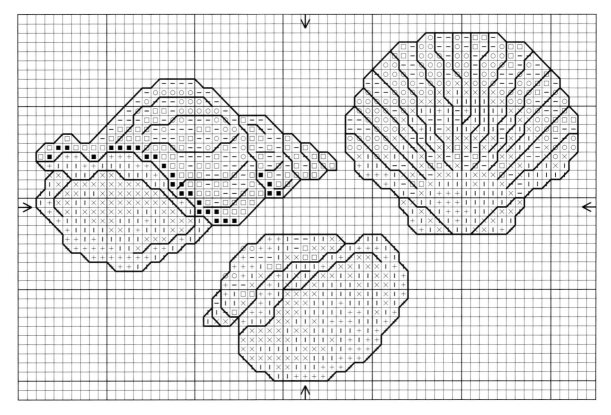

▽ Chart B

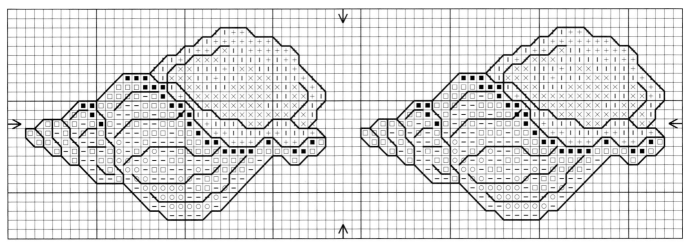

PICTURE

1 Mark the center of the Aida fabric with basting.

2 Begin stitching from the center out, using two strands for cross stitch and one for backstitch (chart A). Work each stitch over one fabric block.

3 When completed, remove the basting and with a cool iron gently press the design from the wrong side.

4 Either frame the design yourself or take to a professional.

GUEST TOWEL

1 Fold the towel in half and stitch a line of basting across the Aida panel, marking the vertical center. Using a tape measure, mark the horizontal center with basting.

Above: These seashell towels are perfect for a guest bathroom.

2 Using two strands for cross stitch and one for backstitch, begin stitching from the center out (chart B). Then repeat the motif along the band, leaving a gap of four blocks between each shell.

3 When all the stitching has been completed, remove the basting. With a cool iron, gently press the design from the wrong side.

TIP

Do ensure all the loose thread ends are very firmly secured; otherwise, they may work loose when the towel is washed or used.

Windmill pantry

Inspired by the rustic scenes on Delft pottery, these humble little windmills will really brighten up a plain pantry. With a smart shelf edging and trendy patches stitched onto kitchen accessories, the clear blue motifs add a slightly nostalgic quality to your kitchen.

SKILL LEVEL: 1

MEASUREMENTS

Worked on 14-count Aida with each cross stitch worked over one fabric block, the dish towel patch motif measures 2½ x 1½ in. (6 x 4 cm.). Worked on 18-count Aida with each cross stitch worked over one fabric block, the shelf edging motif (which is repeated to fit the desired length) measures 4¾ x 1¼ in.(5 x 3 cm.).

YOU WILL NEED

For the embroidery
- 8 in. (20 cm.) white 18-count Aida, divided by the shelf length plus 1½ in. (4 cm.)
- Two 5½ in.(14 cm.) squares white 14-count Aida
- Tapestry needle, size 26
- Embroidery hoop
- Scissors
- Contrasting basting thread
- DMC stranded cottons as listed

To make up the projects
- Basic sewing kit
- Sewing machine (optional)
- White sewing thread
- Acrylic fridge magnet

	Color	Shade	No. of skeins
■	dark blue	796	1
■	royal blue	798	1
□	baby blue	809	1

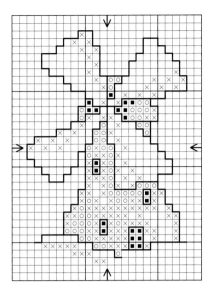

△ Chart A

DISH TOWEL PATCH

1 Fold the 14-count Aida in half horizontally and vertically, pressing firmly on the folds to form strong creases.

2 With contrasting floss, stitch a line of basting along each crease to mark the fabric center. Begin stitching from the center out, using two strands for cross stitch and one for backstitch (chart A). Work over one fabric block.

3 When you have completed the stitching, press the design gently on the reverse.

4 Fold over ¼ in. (1 cm.) all the way round, then pin and baste to make a simple square patch.

5 Position the patch onto the dish towel, then pin and baste in place. Using either a sewing machine or slipstitching by hand, secure the patch to the dish towel and remove all the basting thread.

Symbol	Color	Backstitch	Shade
■	dark blue	◩	796
○	royal blue		798
✕	baby blue		809

Above: The patch could also be stitched onto an apron.

▽ Chart B

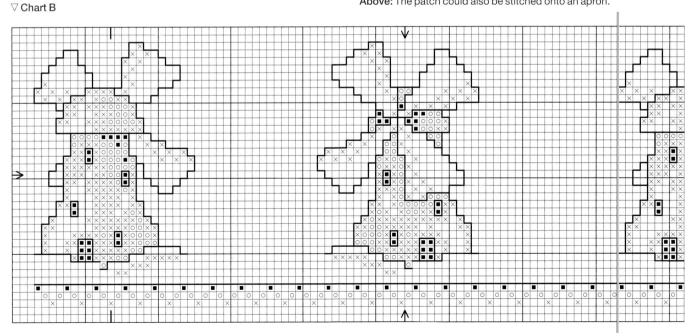

overlap pattern from this point ▷

SHELF EDGING

1 Measure the length of your shelf and cut a piece of 18-count Aida 8 in. (20 cm.) wide by the shelf length, plus 1½ in. (4 cm.).

2 Mark the center with basting.

3 Using one strand of floss for all stitches and working over one fabric block, begin stitching from the center out (chart B). Repeat the design along the length of the fabric, finishing with a complete motif at least 2 in. (5 cm.) from either end.

4 When complete, press gently on the reverse. Then, seven blocks from the base of the stitching, fold the bottom third of the fabric behind the embroidery and baste in place. Either machine or hand stitch above and below the design along the length of the fabric.

5 On either side of the design, turn 1 in. (2 cm.) under and secure.

6 Turn the top third of the fabric over and press firmly to create a strong fold.

7 Finally, using double-sided tape or staples, attach the top part of the fabric to the top of the shelf, letting the windmill border hang down at right angles.

MAGNET

1 Stitch as for the patch and make up the magnet using the supplier's directions.

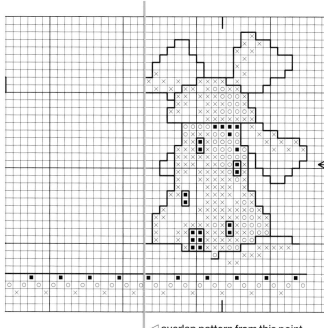

◁ overlap pattern from this point

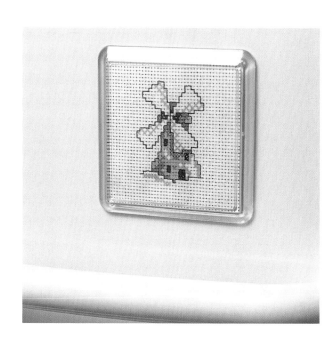

Green linen tea set

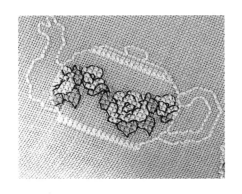

Use these lovely tea set motifs to create something special to accompany your favorite china at teatime. Using backstitch to draw the outlines and cross stitch to create the patterns adds an interesting design twist.

SKILL LEVEL: **2**

MEASUREMENTS
Worked on E3609 linen with each cross stitch worked over two fabric threads, the tray cloth motif (which is repeated) measures 6 x 1½ in. (15 x 4 cm.). The napkin motif measures 2½ x 1½ in. (6.5 x 4 cm.) and the napkin ring motif measures 3½ x ¾ in. (9 x 2 cm.).

YOU WILL NEED
For the embroidery
- 20 x 13 in. (50 x 33 cm.) pale green E3609 Belfast linen
- 6 x 6 in. (15 x 15 cm.) pale green E3609 Belfast linen
- 13 x 13 in. (32 x 32 cm.) white E3609 Belfast linen
- Tapestry needle, size 26
- Embroidery hoop
- Scissors
- Contrasting basting thread
- DMC stranded cottons as listed

To make up the projects
- Sewing machine
- Pins
- Matching sewing thread
- 10 ft. (3 m.) white bias binding
- Acrylic napkin ring

Color	Shade	No. of skeins
pale green	164	1
forest green	520	1
white	blanc	1

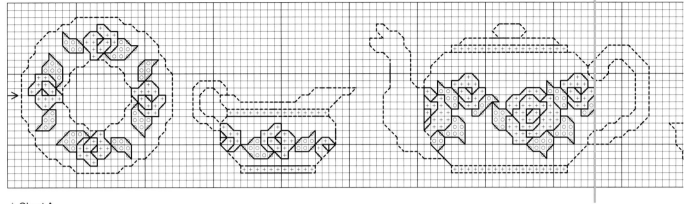

△ Chart A

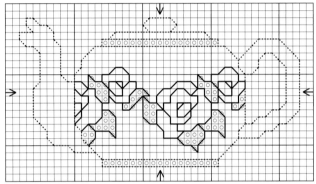

△ Chart B

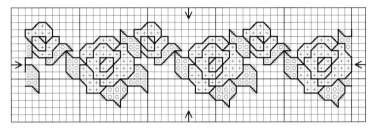

△ Chart C

Below: White floss on pale green linen creates an unusual effect.

Symbol	Color	Backstitch	Shade
○	pale green	⬚	164
	forest green	◩	520
+	white	◪	blanc

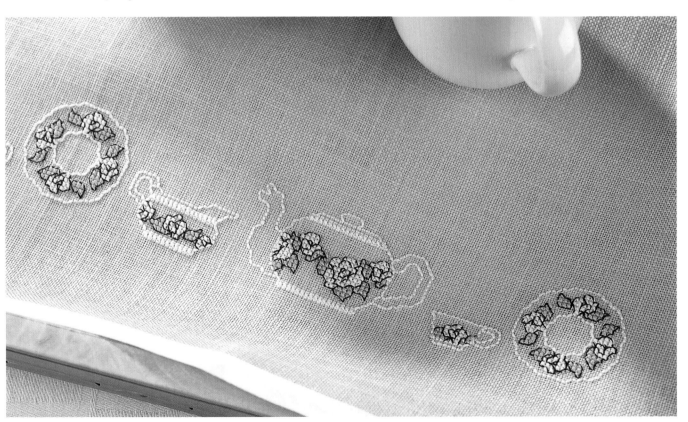

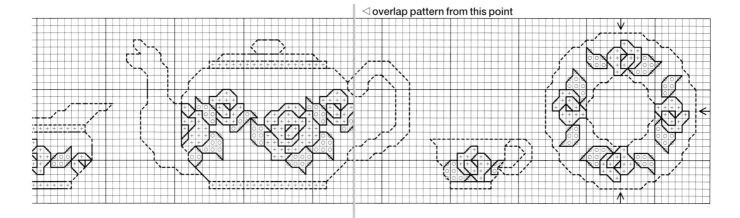

TRAY CLOTH

1 Cut a 20 x 13 in. (50 x 33 cm.) piece of pale green linen and bind the edges with white bias binding.

2 Fold the cloth in half across the width and stitch a line of basting to mark the vertical center. Next, stitch another line of basting 2½ in. (6 cm.) from the bottom of the cloth. Where the lines cross, marks the central and starting point.

3 Stitch from the center out, using two strands of floss for cross stitch and the white backstitch, but only one strand for backstitch worked in dark green. Work each stitch over two fabric threads (chart A).

4 Using the center marks on the chart, stitch the left side of the design first, then repeat to the right.

5 Once you have completed the stitching, remove the central basting and using a cool iron, press gently.

NAPKIN

1 Cut a 13 in. (32 cm.) square of white linen and bind the edges as for the tray cloth.

2 Baste two lines about 2 in. (5 cm.) in from the left side and the bottom edge of the napkin. Using where the lines cross as the central mark, work each stitch over two fabric threads (chart B).

3 Use two strands of floss for cross stitch and pale green backstitch and one strand for the dark green backstitch.

4 Remove the basting and gently press with a cool iron.

NAPKIN RING

1 Cut a small piece of the pale green linen 3¼ x 6 in. (8 x 15 cm.), marking the center with basting.

2 Stitching from the center out, use two strands for cross stitch and one strand for backstitch. Work each stitch over two fabric threads (chart C).

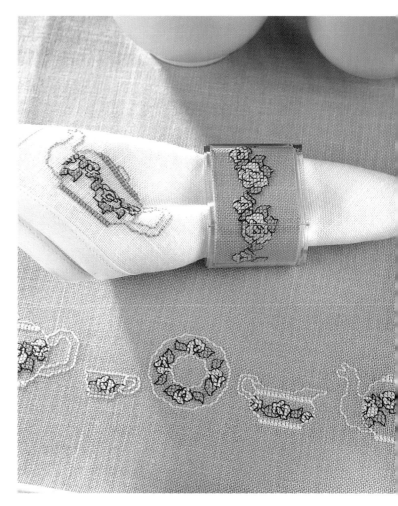

Above: Use this charming tea set for special guests.

3 When complete, back with Vilene and make up the napkin ring using the supplier's directions.

TIP

The attractive rose border could be repeated along a linen band to adorn any number of teatime accessories, such as a dish towel, tea cozy, or even an apron.

Gingham playmat and pram toys

Soft pastel shades of gingham in simple nursery shapes create something different for your new arrival. A soft patchwork play mat and some jingling pram toys will welcome your newborn girls and boys.

SKILL LEVEL: 2

MEASUREMENTS

Worked on 11-count Aida with each cross stitch worked over one fabric block, the playmat motifs measure 2½ x 2½ in. (6 x 6 cm.). Worked on 14-count Aida with each cross stitch worked over one fabric block, the toy motifs measure 2 x 2 in. (5 x 5 cm.).

YOU WILL NEED

For the embroidery
- Three 7 x 7 in. (18 x 18 cm.) squares 11-count white Aida
- Three 5 x 5 in. (12 x 12 cm.) squares 14-count white Aida
- Tapestry needle, size 24
- Tapestry needle, size 26
- Embroidery hoop
- Embroidery scissors
- Contrasting basting thread
- DMC stranded cottons as listed

To make up the projects
- Basic sewing kit
- Sewing machine
- White sewing thread
- 40 in. (1 m.) blue gingham
- 20 in. (50 cm.) yellow gingham
- 30 x 18 in. (75 x 45 cm.) medium weight batting
- Fabric pen
- 3 x small bells
- 47 in. (1.2 m .) cord

Color		Shade	No. of skeins
☐	lemon	745	1
☐	baby blue	813	1
☐	pale sky	827	1
☐	light green	913	1
☐	palest mint	955	1
☐	baby pink	963	1
☐	candy pink	3326	1
☐	tangerine	3855	1

PATCHWORK PLAY MAT

1 Baste down the center of the 11-count Aida squares.

2 With the size 24 needle and working each stitch over one fabric block, use three strands for cross stitch and two for backstitch. Stitch one of each motif in the middle of each square. When completed, remove the basting and gently press with a cool iron.

3 Cut eight 7 in. (18 cm.) squares from the blue gingham and four from the yellow gingham.

4 With the three stitched squares, arrange them into a checkered pattern, three squares across and five down.

5 Taking a ¾ in. (1.5 cm.) seam allowance, stitch the squares together in horizontal strips, three at a time.

6 When you have five strips, iron the seams open and stitch the strips together, taking care to match the seams.

7 Cut a piece of backing fabric measuring 32 x 20 in. (81 x 51 cm.) and place it together with the patchwork right sides facing. Put the batting on the wrong side of the backing fabric and stitch all round, basting a ⅗ in. (1.5 cm.) seam allowance and leaving a 8 in. (20 cm.) gap down one side to turn through.

8 Trim the batting from all edges and corners. Turn right sides out and slipstitch the gap shut. Then carefully machine down the patchwork seams to create a quilted effect.

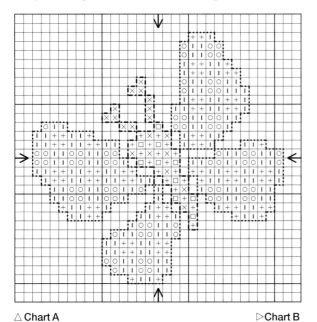

△ Chart A ▷Chart B

▽ Chart C

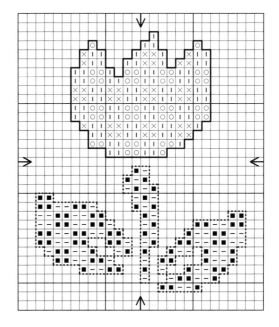

Symbol	Color	Backstitch	Shade
+	lemon		745
▲	baby blue	◥	813
×	pale sky		827
■	light green	◥	913
−	palest mint		955
I	baby pink		963
○	candy pink	⠡	3326
□	tangerine	◥	3855

Above: The gingham fabric is echoed in the motif.

PRAM TOYS

1 Baste down the center of the 14-count Aida squares.
2 With the size 26 needle and working each stitch over one fabric block, use two strands for cross stitch and one for backstitch.

3 Stitch one of each motif in the middle of each square. When complete, remove the basting and gently press with a cool iron.
4 Cut three circles each measuring 4 in. (10 cm.) in diameter and three diagonal strips 12 in. (30 cm.) long and 1½ in. (4 cm.) wide from the coordinating fabrics.
5 Fold the strips in half lengthwise, then pin and baste them around the three circles, fold toward the center.
6 Cut the stitched sample into circles measuring 4 in. (10 cm.) in diameter. Then, with the fabric strips and embroidery on the inside pin, baste and stitch the circles together, leaving a 1½ in. (4 cm.) gap in each one to turn through.
7 Turn the pads right side out and gently press with a cool iron. Fill with batting and place a single bell within, then slipstitch the gap shut.
8 Take a length of cord and with a needle and thread, stitch the pads onto it at equal intervals.

TIP

If you were stitching this project as a gift, you could use one of the motifs on a card to accompany your present.

Above: Stitched onto a length of cord, these pads are lovely toys when tied across a pram.

Architectural drawing

These classical building studies are worked in shades of gray to give them the drawn quality of architectural charcoal sketches. Stitch this motif onto an address book cover to make a really good impression in your entrance hall. An elegantly framed picture adds a classical feel.

SKILL LEVEL: 3

MEASUREMENTS
Worked on Brittney evenweave and with each cross stitch worked over two fabric threads, the picture motif measures 5½ x 4½ in. (13.5 x 11.5 cm.). The address book motif measures 2½ x 2 in. (6 x 5 cm.).

YOU WILL NEED
For the embroidery
- 10 x 10 in. (25 x 25 cm.) white E3270 Brittney evenweave
- 5½ x 5½ in. (14 x 14 cm.) white E3270 Brittney evenweave
- Tapestry needle, size 26
- Embroidery hoop
- Scissors
- Contrasting basting thread
- DMC stranded cottons as listed

To make up the projects
- Address book
- 10 in. (25 cm.) square frame
- Fabric glue or double-sided transparent tape

Color	Shade	No. of skeins
mid gray	318	2
charcoal	413	1
slate gray	414	1
silver gray	415	2
palest gray	762	2
darkest gray	3799	2
white	blanc	1

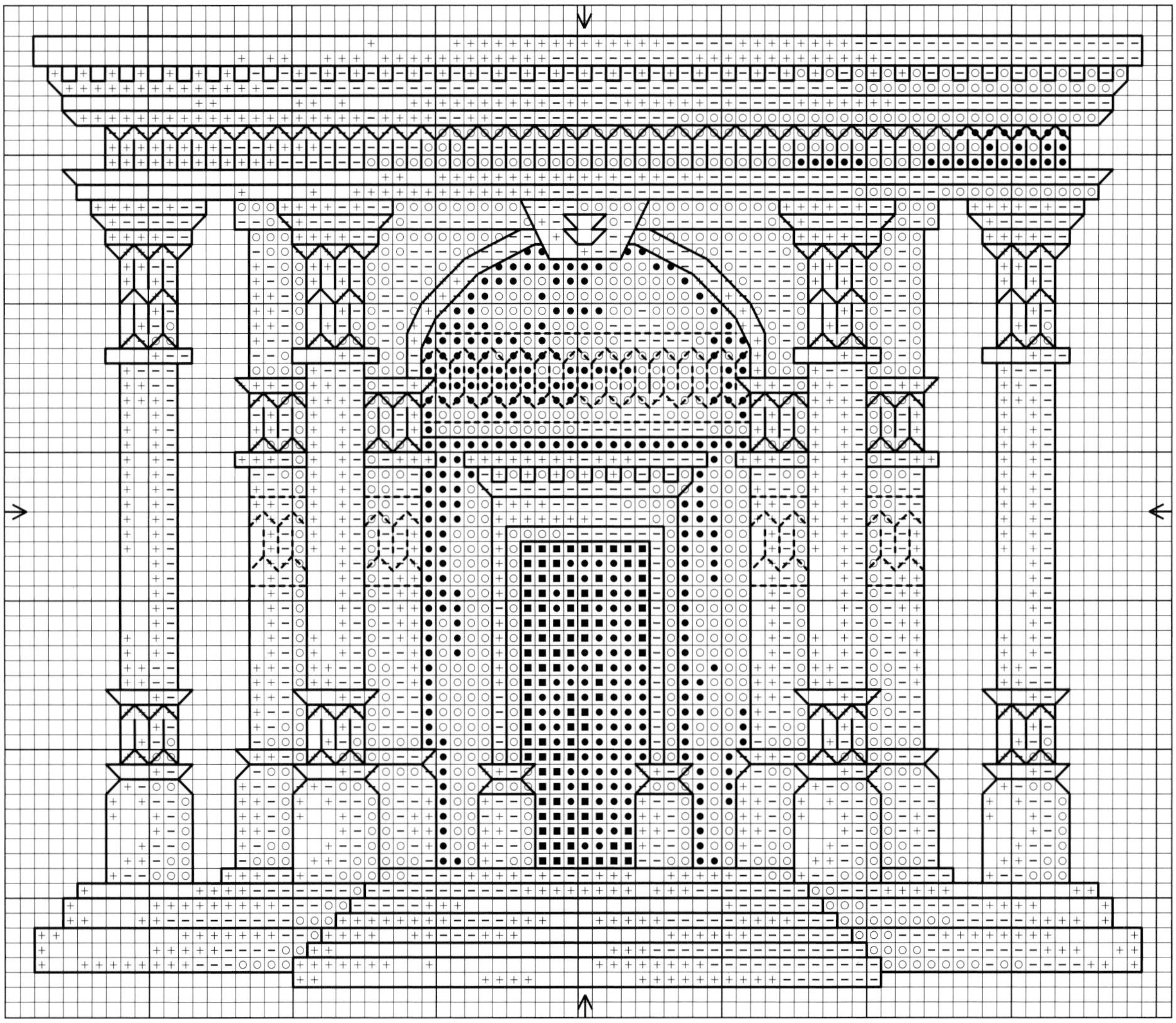

△ Chart A

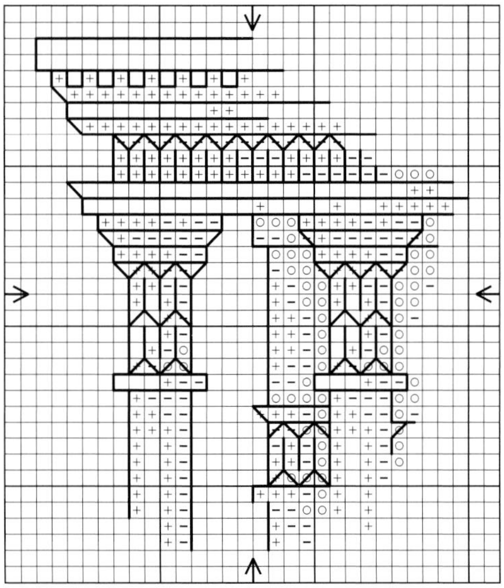

△ Chart B

Symbol	Color	Backstitch	Shade
○	mid gray		318
■	charcoal		413
●	slate gray		414
−	silver gray		415
+	palest gray		762
	darkest gray		3799
	white		blanc

PICTURE

1 Cut a 10 in. (25 cm.) square of white evenweave. Mark the center with basting.

2 Begin stitching from the center out, working over two fabric threads, using two strands for cross stitch and one for backstitch (chart A).

3 When complete, remove the basting and press the design gently on the reverse with a cool iron.

4 To finish, frame the design yourself or take to a professional.

ADDRESS BOOK

1 Cut a 5½ in. (14 cm.) square of white evenweave. Mark the center with basting.

2 Begin stitching from the center out, working over two fabric threads and using two strands for cross stitch and one for backstitch (chart B).

3 When you have completed the stitching, remove the basting and press the design gently on the reverse with a cool iron.

4 Trim the design to leave 1 in. (2 cm.) of unworked fabric all the way round the motif. Then fray the edges by carefully pulling out the end six fabric threads one at a time on all four sides.

5 Leave three threads in place, then pull out one more thread to form a border pattern around the edge.

6 Using double-sided tape or fabric glue, secure the design in place on the front of the address book.

TIP

These designs are shown in shades of gray, but if you would prefer a softer image, why not pick some corresponding shades in sepia tones for an antique print appearance.

Above: Using several shades of gray adds depth and definition to the motif.

Left: The notebook shows just a small section of the main design.

Japanese lady

This elegant Japanese woman glancing shyly over her fan is reminiscent of the prints and drawings of ancient Japan. With blocks of color and bold outlines, I have tried to recreate this old style, leaving the hands, face, and fan unstitched for a printlike quality.

SKILL LEVEL: 3
(quarter and three-quarter stitches used)

MEASUREMENTS
Worked on 28-count Quaker cloth with each cross stitch worked over two fabric threads, the picture motif measures 6 x 3 in. (16 x 8 cm.). The blossom motif measures 2½ x 2½ in. (6.5 x 6.5 cm.).

YOU WILL NEED
For the embroidery
- 8 x 12 in. (20 x 30 cm.) 28-count white Quaker cloth
- 7 x 7 in. (18 x 18 cm.) 28-count white Quaker cloth
- Tapestry needle, size 26
- Embroidery hoop
- Scissors
- Contrasting basting thread
- DMC stranded cottons as listed

To make up the projects
- Basic sewing kit
- Silver bowl
- Frame

Color		Shade	No. of skeins
■	black	310	1
☐	soft aqua	3761	1
☐	sand	676	1
■	dark gray	413	1
☐	candy pink	962	1
■	cerise	309	1
☐	pale pink	963	1
■	gray blue	931	1

PICTURE

1 Fold the piece of 12 x 8 in. (30 x 20 cm.) evenweave in half horizontally and vertically.

2 With contrasting cotton, stitch a line of basting along each crease to mark the fabric center.

3 Begin stitching from the center out, using two strands for cross stitch and one for backstitch. Work each stitch over two fabric threads.

4 When all the stitching has been completed, remove the basting and with a cool iron, gently press the design from the wrong side.

5 Either frame the design yourself or take to a professional.

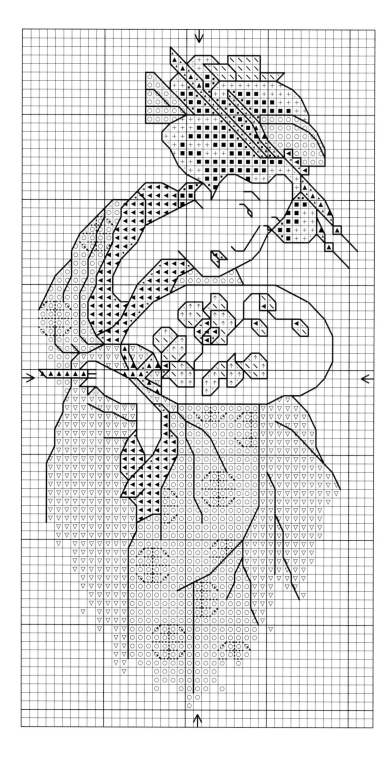

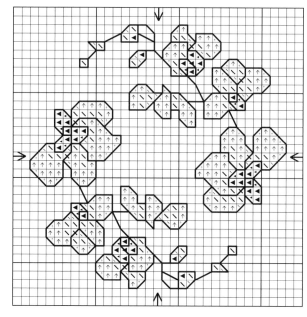

◁ Chart A   △ Chart B

Symbol	Color	Backstitch	Shade
■	black	◥	310
○	soft aqua		3761
▲	sand		676
+	dark gray		413
＼	candy pink		962
◀	cerise		309
↑	pale pink		963
▽	gray blue	◥	931

Left: Choose a frame that complements the colors in the design.

Below: The black backstitch gives the motif definition.

SILVER BOWL

1 Mark the fabric center with basting.

2 Begin stitching from the center out, using two strands for cross stitch and one for backstitch. Work each stitch over two fabric threads.

3 When complete, remove the basting and press the design from the wrong side.

4 Finally, following the supplier's directions, fit the finished design into the bowl lid.

Animal Motifs

Here we show the lighter side of life with some simple
animal, fish, and bird designs. You can adorn your kitchen
accessories with quirky farmyard silhouettes, or make eating
at the table fun for children with some comic cat tablemats.

Farmyard animals

Bring a touch of humor to your cooking with these farmyard silhouette kitchen accessories. In dramatic black and white, they are the sillier side of chic. Stitched in a row across an Aida band or on a patch, they are simple to create and easy to attach.

SKILL LEVEL: 1

MEASUREMENTS

The dish towel motif (which is repeated to create a border) measures 7½ x 1¾ in. (19 x 4.5 cm.). Worked on 14-count Aida with each cross stitch worked over one fabric block, the apron patch motif measures 4½ x 3 in. (11 x 8 cm.). Worked on 11-count Aida with each cross stitch worked over one fabric block, the oven pad motif measures 3 x 2½ in. (8 x 7 cm.).

YOU WILL NEED

For the embroidery
- 5 x 5 in. (12 x 12 cm.) 11-count white Aida
- 6 x 5 in. (15 x 12 cm.) 14-count white Aida
- 2 in. (5 cm.) Aida band (dish towel width)
- Tapestry needle, size 26
- Embroidery hoop
- Scissors
- Contrasting basting thread
- Soft pencil
- DMC stranded cottons as listed

To make up the projects
- Basic sewing kit
- Sewing machine
- Matching sewing thread
- Chenille needle, size 26

- Plain dish towel
- Oven pad
- Apron

Color		Shade	No. of skeins
■	black	310	2

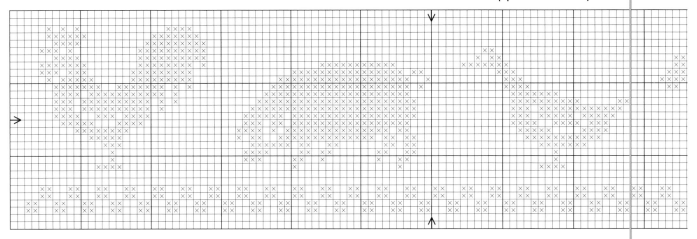

Symbol	Color	Backstitch	Shade
☒	black	◨	310

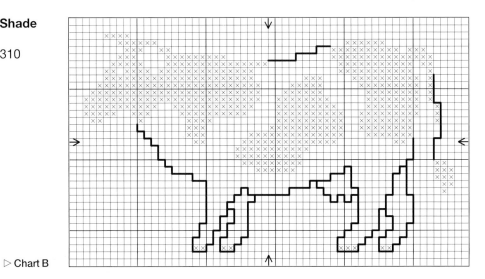

▷ Chart B

TOWEL BAND

1 To calculate the amount of Aida band you will need, measure the width of your dish towel and add 1 in. (2 cm.).

2 Fold the band in half and, using a contrasting color, mark the center with a line of basting. Fold lengthwise to find the horizontal center and baste another short line. Where the lines cross, marks the center and starting point.

3 Work each stitch over one fabric block, using two strands of cotton for cross stitch (chart A).

4 Repeat the design along the band, finishing with a complete motif at least 1½ in. (4 cm.) from either end.

5 Remove the basting and then, using a cool iron, press the band gently. Position the Aida band on the dish towel, then pin and baste in place.

6 Finally, either machine or slip stitch in place, remembering to turn under the end of the band to keep it neat.

Below: Black and white silhouettes are simple but stylish.

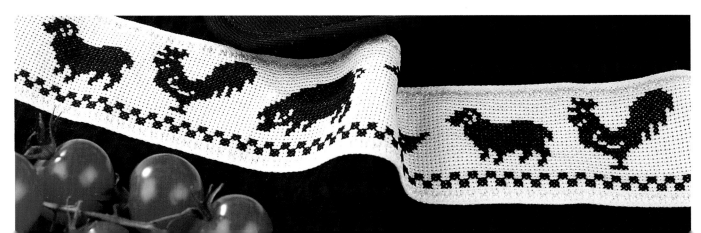

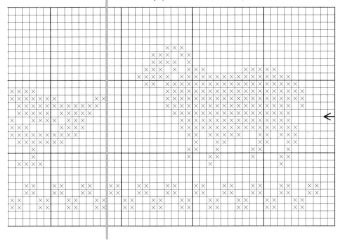

◁ overlap pattern from this point

Above and below: The fun animal patches are easy to stitch and attach.

COW APRON PATCH

1 Cut a piece of 14-count white Aida 6 x 5 in. (15 x 12 cm.) and mark the center with basting.

2 Using two strands of cotton for both cross stitch and backstitch, work over one fabric block (chart B).

3 Fold over ½ in. (1 cm.) on all sides. Position the patch on the apron, then pin and baste in place.

4 Using the chenille needle and two strands of black stranded cotton, backstitch the patch to the apron three fabric blocks from the fold line.

5 Finally, remove all basting and gently press on the reverse using a cool iron.

COCKEREL OVEN PAD

1 Pick one of the small animal silhouettes from chart A. Using a soft pencil, mark the center of your chosen motif on the chart.

2 Cut a 5 in. (12 cm.) square of 11-count Aida and mark the center.

3 Using three strands of floss for the cross stitch, work over one fabric block.

4 Count seven fabric blocks from the design and fold over the excess on all sides.

5 Position the patch on the oven pad, then pin and baste in place. Using the chenille needle and two strands of black stranded cotton, backstitch the patch to the apron three fabric blocks from the fold line.

6 Finally remove all the basting and gently press on the reverse using a cool iron.

TIP

When stitching patches to pockets, do remember to stitch through only one fabric layer, or your pocket will be unusable.

Cute cats breakfast set

Breakfast takes on a whole new meaning with this fun table set for children—entice them to the breakfast table with these lovely comic cat accessories. An Aida tablemat, mug, and coaster will really brighten up the day.

SKILL LEVEL: 1

MEASUREMENTS

Worked on 11-count Aida with each cross stitch worked over one fabric block, the place mat motif measures 5½ x 4 in. (14 x 10 cm.) and the coaster motif measures 2 x 1½ in. (5 x 4 cm.). Worked on 14-count Aida with each cross stitch worked over one fabric block, the mug motif measures 4½ x 3 in. (12 x 8 cm.).

YOU WILL NEED
For the embroidery
- 16 x 14 in. (40 x 35 cm.) pale blue 11-count Aida
- 10 x 5 in. (25 x 12 cm.) pale blue 14-count Aida
- 6 x 6 in. (15 x 15 cm.) pale blue 11-count Aida
- Tapestry needle, size 26
- Embroidery hoop
- Scissors
- Contrasting basting thread
- DMC stranded cottons as listed

To make up the projects
- Basic sewing kit
- Sewing machine (optional)
- Matching sewing thread
- Vilene
- Acrylic mug
- Acrylic coaster

Color		Shade	No. of skeins
■	black	310	1
☐	pale pink	605	1
■	orange	722	1
■	ginger	921	1
■	blue	3838	1
☐	white	blanc	1

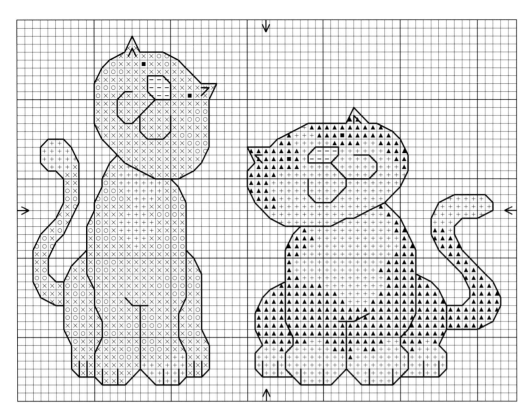

Right: The cats on this place mat really stand out on this pale blue fabric.

◁ **Chart A**

Symbol	Color	Backstitch	Shade
■	black	◺	310
−	pale pink		605
✕	orange		722
○	ginger		921
▲	blue		3838
+	white		blanc

PLACE MAT

1 You will need a piece of 11-count pale blue Aida fabric, about 16 x 14 in. (40 x 35 cm.). Hem the fabric by folding over ¼ in. (1 cm.) and then another ½ in. (1.5 cm.). Either machine stitch or hand stitch in place with matching floss.

2 In the bottom left corner, stitch two lines of basting, one horizontally 3 in. (7 cm.) up from the bottom edge, the other vertically 3½ in. (9 cm.) in from the left. Use the point where they cross as the design center.

3 Work each stitch over one fabric block, using three strands of floss for the cross stitch and two for the backstitch (chart A).

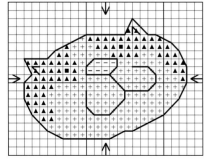

△ **Chart B**

Left: Acrylic coasters are easy to make up.

4 When complete, remove the basting and gently press on the reverse with a cool iron.

COASTER

1 For the coaster, simply stitch one of the cat's heads (chart B).
2 Cut a small piece of 11-count pale blue Aida, 6 in. (15 cm.) square and mark the center with basting.
3 Stitch the motif using three strands of floss for the cross stitch and two for the backstitch.
4 When complete, remove the basting and back with Vilene. Then follow the supplier's directions to make up the coaster.

MUG

1 Mark the center of a piece of 14-count pale blue Aida measuring 10 x 5 in. (25 x 12 cm.) with basting stitches.
2 Working from the center out, begin stitching using two strands for cross stitch and one for backstitch.
3 When complete, remove the basting and gently press with a cool iron on the reverse. Back with Vilene and make up the mug using supplier's directions.

Above and below: The place mat and mug will appeal to all children.

Teddy Bear baby set

While awaiting a new arrival, why not fill the time by preparing a few simple gifts? This cozy blanket will be cherished by mother and baby on all those late-night feeds, and as the child grows, this bib will not only look nice but be useful too. A teddy bear rattle with three matching cross stitch hearts is hard to resist.

SKILL LEVEL: 1

MEASUREMENTS
Worked on 11-count Aida with each cross stitch worked over one fabric block, the blanket patch motif measures 4½ x 4 in. (12 x 10 cm.). The bib motif measures 3 x 2½ in. (7.5 x 6 cm.) and the rattle motif measures 1 x ¼ in. (3 x 1 cm.).

YOU WILL NEED
For the embroidery
• Aida bib
• "Ready to Stitch" Teddy rattle
• 6½ x 6 in. (16 x 15 cm.) white 11-count Aida
• Tapestry needle, size 26
• Embroidery hoop
• Scissors
• Contrasting basting thread
• DMC stranded cottons as listed

To make up the projects
• Basic sewing kit
• Sewing machine (optional)
• White sewing thread

Color		Shade	No. of skeins
	coral	351	1
	pale peach	353	1
	dark brown	433	1
	golden brown	436	1
	light brown	437	1
	light tan	739	1
	baby blue	3839	1
	pale sky	3840	1

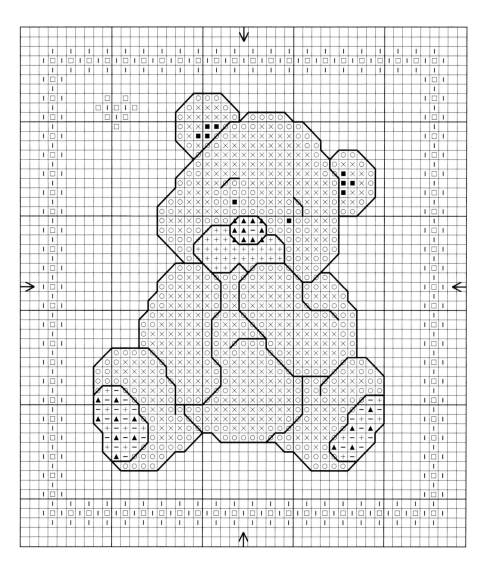

◁ Chart A

▽ Chart B

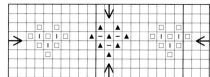

Symbol	Color	Backstitch	Shade
▲	coral		351
−	pale peach		353
■	dark brown	◨	433
○	golden brown		436
⊠	light brown		437
+	light tan		739
▣	baby blue		3839
Ⅰ	pale sky		3840

Right: This teddy bear patch is perfect for a cozy blanket.

BLANKET PATCH

1 Mark the center of the Aida with basting.

2 Begin stitching from the center out, using three strands for cross stitch and two for backstitch. Work each stitch over one fabric block (chart A).

3 When you have completed the design, gently press on the reverse using a cool iron.

4 Count five fabric blocks from the design and fold over the excess Aida on all sides.

5 Position the patch on the blanket. Pin and baste in place.

6 Finally, using either machine or hand stitch, secure the Aida patch to the blanket and remove all the basting.

AIDA BIB

1 Find the bib center by folding it in half horizontally and vertically. With contrasting floss, stitch a line of basting along each crease to mark the center.

Above: Ready-made Aida items are ideal for making up quick gifts.

2 Omitting the border and little heart, begin stitching from the center out. Use two strands for the cross stitch and one for the backstitch, working each stitch over one fabric block.

3 Remove the basting and gently press with a cool iron.

'READY TO STITCH' TEDDY RATTLE

1 Using a tape measure, find the center of the teddy's bib and mark with basting.

2 Stitch the three tiny heart shapes (chart B), using two strands for cross stitch. Work each stitch over one fabric block.

3 When the stitching is complete, remove the basting.

Blue bird bed linen

Blue and white is a classic color combination that works every time—particularly in bedrooms. This crisp white bed linen features swooping blue birds stitched onto pillowcases using waste canvas, as well as on the Aida band on the sheet. A bedside trinket box for precious items is adorned with two birds.

SKILL LEVEL: 1

MEASUREMENTS
Worked on 14-count waste canvas, the pillow motif measures (2½ x 1½ in.) (6 x 4 cm.). The sheet motif (which is repeated to create a border) measures 4½ x 2 in. (11 x 5 cm.). Worked on Hardanger with each cross stitch worked over one pair of threads, the box motif measures 3 x 1¼ in. (7.5 x 3 cm.).

YOU WILL NEED
For the embroidery
- Two 4 in. (10 cm.) squares 14-count waste canvas
- 3 in. (7.5 cm.) Aida band (sheet width)
- 6 x 4 in. (15 x 10 cm.) white Hardanger
- Tapestry needle, size 26
- Chenille needle, size 26
- Embroidery hoop
- Scissors
- Contrasting basting thread
- DMC stranded cottons as listed

To make up the projects
- Basic sewing kit
- Tweezers
- Sewing machine
- White sewing thread

Color		Shade	No. of skeins
▨	soft blue	3839	1
▢	pale sky	3840	2

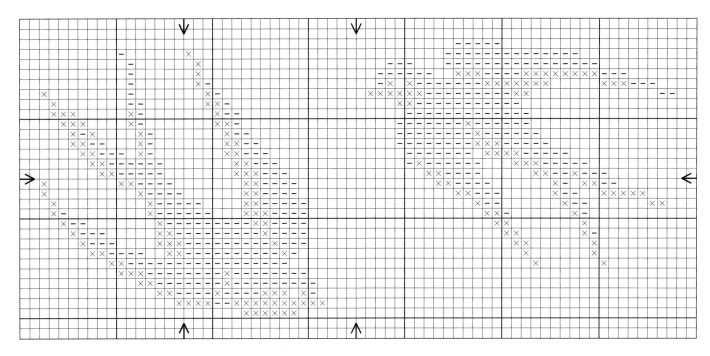

Symbol	Color	Shade
☒	soft blue	3839
☐	pale sky	3840

SHEET BAND

1 To calculate the amount of Aida band you will need, measure the width of your sheet and add 2 in. (5 cm.).

2 Fold the band in half and mark the center with a line of basting. Fold lengthwise to find the horizontal center and baste another short line. Where the lines cross, marks the center and starting point.

3 Using two lengths of stranded cotton in the tapestry needle, cross stitch the first motif from the center out.

4 Leaving four Aida blocks between each motif, continue left and right along the band until you have about 6 in. (15 cm.) clear at either end. (As long as each gap is the same, you can leave larger spaces between each motif to achieve an airier look.)

5 Once you have completed the stitching, remove the basting and use a cool iron to press the band. Pin and baste the band about 2 in. (5 cm.) from the top of the sheet, with the design upside down so that when the sheet is turned over, it will read the correct way.

6 Finally, machine or slip stitch in place, remembering to turn in the end of the band to keep it neat.

Left: The motifs are spaced evenly along the Aida band.

PILLOW CASES

1 Cut a 4 in. (10 cm.) square of waste canvas and mark the center.

2 Position the canvas where you want your bird motif to be, then baste into place, remembering to stitch through only one side of the case.

3 Use a small embroidery hoop to keep the canvas and pillow case layer taut. Stitch using two strands of floss and the chenille needle.

4 When the motif is complete, remove the basting and damp down the waste canvas. Pull the canvas threads out one at a time using tweezers and then gently press with a cool iron.

VARIATION

To add interest to your bedding, you could stitch the motifs in white on a coordinating blue pillowcase.

JEWELRY BOX

1 Mark the center of the Hardanger with basting. Using the center arrows on the chart, work from the center out.

2 Use one length of stranded cotton over one pair of Hardanger threads.

3 When you have completed the stitching, remove the basting and gently press.

4 Make up the box pad using the supplier's directions.

Above: Choose a contrasting color for the second pillowcase.

Right: This little box is perfect for special trinkets and secret items.

Seaside bathroom

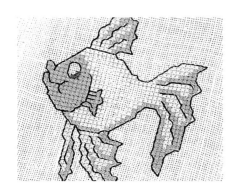

Jazz up your bathtime with these colorful accessories featuring a happy purple sea horse and jolly turquoise fish. Simple patches on color-coordinating towels look really fresh and modern. You could also invest in some acrylic accessories and give your whole bathroom an ocean theme.

SKILL LEVEL: 2

MEASUREMENTS
Worked on 32-count linen with each cross stitch worked over two fabric threads, the motifs measure 3 x 2 ¾ in. (8 x 7 cm.) and 3½ x 2 in. (9 x 4.5 cm.).

YOU WILL NEED
For the embroidery
- Four 6 in. (15 cm.) squares baby blue 32-count E3609 Belfast linen
- Tapestry needle, size 26
- Embroidery hoop
- Scissors
- Contrasting basting thread
- DMC stranded cottons as listed

To make up the projects
- Basic sewing kit
- Sewing machine (optional)
- Matching sewing thread
- Acrylic pot
- Acrylic frame

	Color	Shade	No. of skeins
■	dark blue	311	1
■	lilac	341	1
■	turquoise	807	1
■	navy	823	1
■	purple	3746	1
■	pale aqua	3761	1

▷ Chart A

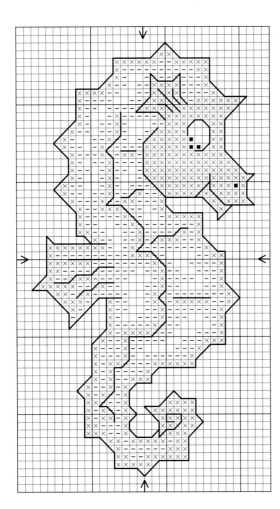

TOWEL PATCHES

1 Fold the linen square in half horizontally and vertically, pressing firmly on the folds to form strong creases. Stitch a line of basting along each crease to mark the fabric center.

2 Begin stitching from the center out, using two strands for cross stitch and one for backstitch. Work over two fabric threads (chart A).

3 When you have completed the stitching, remove the basting and press.

4 Measure ½ in. (1.5 cm.) away from the design and fold over the excess fabric on all sides, pinning and basting in place. This will make up a simple patch.

5 Position the patch on the towel and pin, then baste.

6 Finally, using either a sewing machine or slipstitching by hand, secure the linen to the towel. Remove all the basting thread.

Above: Choose a towel that matches the colors of the motif.

Symbol	Color	Backstitch	Shade
▲	dark blue	↘	311
−	lilac		341
○	turquoise		807
■	navy	↘	823
✕	purple		3746
+	pale aqua		3761

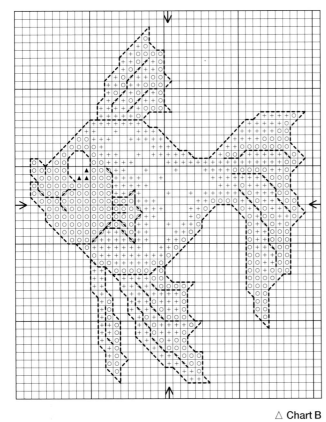

△ Chart B

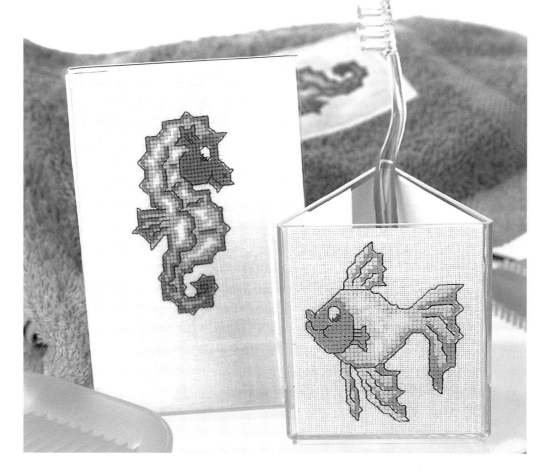

ACRYLIC ACCESSORIES

1 Mark the center of the linen squares with basting.

2 Begin stitching from the center out, using two strands for cross stitch and one for backstitch. Work over two fabric threads (chart B).

3 When the stitching is complete, remove the basting and press the design from the reverse.

4 To finish, back the linen with Vilene to prevent fraying, then trim and make up using the supplier's directions.

TIP

If your bathroom has a specific color scheme, it is easy to change the color of these motifs. Just pick three shades of the same color, making sure the darkest one will give a strong enough outline to pick out the detail.

VARIATION

These fun motifs are perfect if you fancy making your own cards. Simply stitch the motif as above. Trim to ¼ in. (1 cm) all round, then fray the edges and stick onto a blank card.

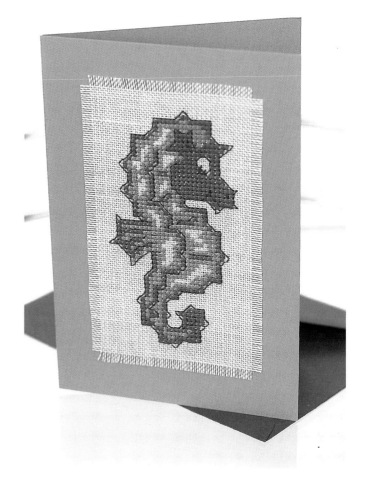

Geometric Motifs

Simple geometric designs are often the most
effective, especially when worked in strong,
contrasting colors. Repeated patterns, whether a
grouping of hearts or a Turkish design, are pleasing
to the eye and will lift a whole range of items, from
table linen to towels.

Blue and white sampler

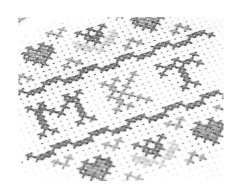

This lovely wall hanging adds a modern touch to the traditional sampler. Stitched in clear blue shades, it has a fresh Scandinavian feel. With a matching notebook and personalized wooden bowl, it would make a lovely gift for a special friend. Simply add your loved one's initials.

SKILL LEVEL: 1

MEASUREMENTS

Worked on Aida band, the wall hanging design measures 6 x 3½ in. (16 x 9 cm.). Worked on 14-count Aida with each cross stitch worked over one fabric block, the wooden pot motif measures 2¾ x 2¾ in. (7 x 7 cm.). Worked on 16-count linen with each cross stitch worked over one fabric thread, the notebook motif measures 4½ x 2½ in. (11 x 6 cm.).

YOU WILL NEED

For the embroidery
- 12 in. (30 cm.) of 5½ in. (14 cm.) wide Aida band
- 5½ in. (14 cm.) 14-count white Aida
- 6 x 4 in. (15 x 10 cm.) 16-count white linen
- Tapestry needle, size 26
- Embroidery hoop
- Scissors
- Contrasting basting thread
- DMC stranded cottons as listed

To make up the projects
- Basic sewing kit
- Sewing machine (optional)
- White sewing thread
- Bell pull rods
- Wooden pot
- Small notebook
- Glue or double-sided tape

Color		Shade	No. of skeins
■	royal blue	798	1
■	light blue	799	1
□	pale sky	800	1

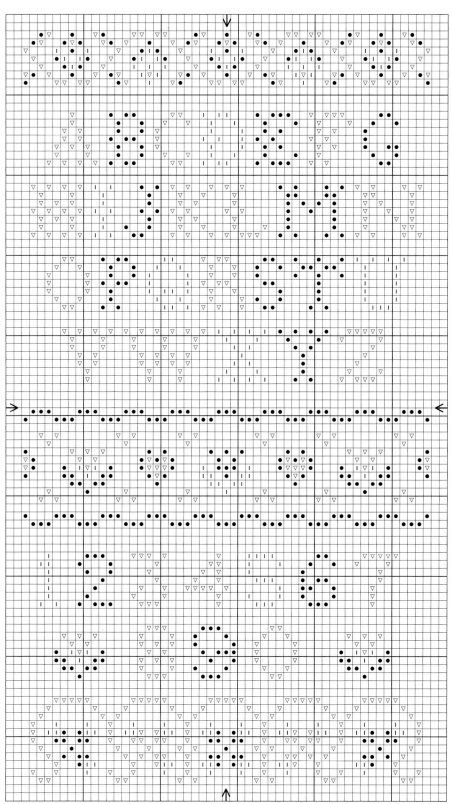

△ Chart A

Symbol	Color	Shade
●	royal blue	798
▽	light blue	799
I	pale sky	800

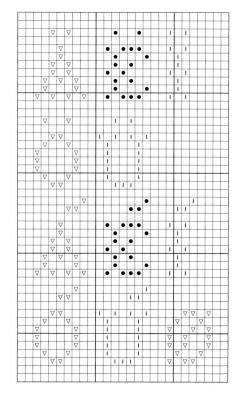

△ **Chart B:** Additional letters and accents are easy to create. Here are some of the most common ones.

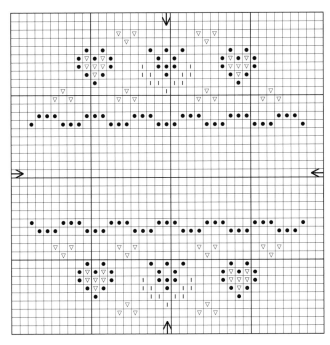

△ Chart C

Above: Add the initials of a loved one for a special gift.

WALL HANGING

1 Fold the Aida band in half vertically and horizontally, then mark the creases with basting. Using two strands of floss in the needle and working over one fabric block, begin stitching from the center out (chart A).

2 When the sampler is complete, remove the basting. With a cool iron, gently press the design on the reverse.

3 Fold over ½ in. (1 cm.), then another 1½ in. (3 cm.) at both ends. Pin and baste, then either machine or hand stitch in place using white sewing thread. This forms the channels through which to slot the bell pull rods.

4 Finally slip the bell pull rods into place and hang.

PERSONALIZED WOODEN BOWL

1 Personalizing the design is easy. Referring to the alphabet on the sampler chart and using a soft pencil, simply draw your chosen initials onto the chart.

2 Fold the Aida in half vertically and horizontally, then mark the creases with basting.

3 Using two strands of floss in the needle and working over one fabric block, begin stitching from the center out (chart C).

4 When you have completed the stitching, remove the basting and gently press the design on the reverse.

5 Make up the pot using the supplier's directions.

Right: Keep all your secrets in this notebook.

NOTEBOOK

1 Mark the center of the linen with basting.

2 Use one strand of floss in the needle and work over one fabric thread. Be careful not to pull your stitches too tight, as they will slip between the weave.

3 Remove the basting and with a cool iron, gently press on the reverse.

4 Trim to ½ in. (1 cm.) outside the design, then pull out a couple of fabric threads to form a fringed edge. Stick the embroidery to the book using glue or tape.

Playing card motifs

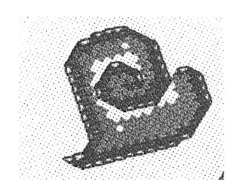

Add a touch of fun to your boudoir with these girly playing card motifs. Stitch the heart, club, diamond, and spade in turn along a band to adorn the top of a sheet, or in a square to patch onto a fluffy cushion. And why not use a single motif to personalize your own notebook?

SKILL LEVEL: 1

MEASUREMENTS

Worked on Aida band with each cross stitch worked over one fabric block, the sheet motif (which is repeated) measures 8 x 1¾ in. (21 x 4 cm.). Worked on 22-count Hardanger with each cross stitch worked over two pairs of threads, the cushion patch motif measures 4½ x 4½ in. (11 x 11 cm.) and the notebook motif measures 2 x 1¾ in. (5 x 4.5 cm.).

YOU WILL NEED

For the embroidery
- 6 x 6 in. (16 x 16 cm.) 22-count white Hardanger
- 5 x 5 in. (12 x 12 cm.) 22-count white Hardanger
- 2 in. (5 cm.) Aida band (sheet width)
- Tapestry needle, size 26
- Tapestry needle, size 24
- Embroidery hoop
- Scissors
- Contrasting basting thread
- Soft pencil
- DMC stranded cottons as listed

To make up the projects
- Basic sewing kit
- Sewing machine
- Matching sewing thread
- Bias binding
- Plain sheet
- Fleece cushion cover

Color		Shade	No. of skeins
■	lavender	155	2
□	lilac	210	2
■	coral	335	2
□	pink	3608	2

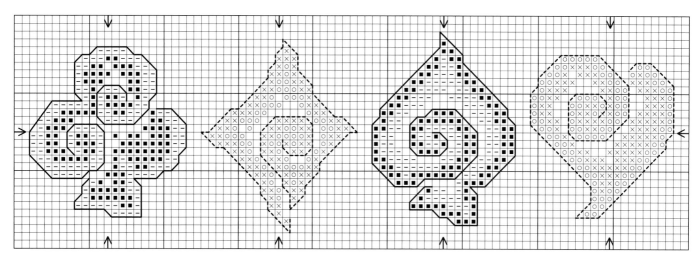

△ Chart A

▽ Chart B

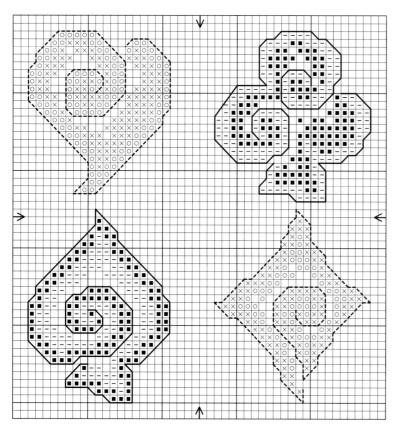

Symbol	Color	Backstitch	Shade
■	lavender	↘	155
−	lilac		210
○	coral	◩	335
⊠	pink		3608

Above: A pretty cushion patch.

CUSHION PATCH

1 Cut a 6½ in. (16 cm.) square of white Hardanger and mark the center with basting.

2 With the size 24 tapestry needle and using four strands of floss in the needle for the cross stitch and two for the backstitch, stitch the design from the center out (chart B). Work each stitch over two pairs of fabric threads.

3 With the motifs complete, remove the basting and gently press on the reverse using a cool iron.

4 Position the stitched square centrally on the cushion cover. Counting six pairs of fabric threads in from the edge, pin and baste, then machine stitch in place.

5 Finally, pull four pairs of fabric threads away on all sides to create a fringed effect around the edge of the patch.

NOTEBOOK

1 Stitch as for cushion patch, using only one motif on a 3 in. (7.5 cm.) square of white Hardanger.

2 Attach to the book, as desired.

Above: Some notebooks have a cut-out panel.

Above: The motifs are evenly spaced along the Aida band.

SHEET BAND

1 To calculate the amount of Aida band you will need, measure the width of your sheet and add 2 in. (5 cm.).

2 Fold the band in half and mark the center with a line of basting. Stitch further lines at 2¼ in. (6 cm.) intervals to either side, continuing along the band.

3 Fold lengthwise to find the horizontal center and baste a series of short lines crossing the first ones. Where the lines cross, marks the center and starting point for each motif.

4 Using two lengths of stranded floss for cross stitch and one for backstitch, work each stitch over one fabric block. Stitch the motifs in turn across the band (*spaces between motifs not shown on chart*).

5 Remove the basting and, using a cool iron, press the band gently on the reverse.

6 Pin and baste the band about 3½ in. (9 cm.) from the top of the sheet, with the design upside down so that when the sheet is turned over it will read correctly. Finally, machine or slip stitch in place, remembering to turn in the ends to keep it neat.

Red and white table linen

Use a simple sampler motif to create some stylish table linens. A red design on crisp white fabric gives this dramatic table runner with matching accessories a touch of modern flare and brightens up your dining table. With hundreds of floss colors to choose from, you could match any color scheme.

SKILL LEVEL: 2

MEASUREMENTS
Worked on 28-count Brittney evenweave with each cross stitch worked over two fabric threads, the table runner motif measures 12½ x 3 in. (32 x 8 cm.). The napkin motif measures 2 x 2 in. (5 x 5 cm.) and the napkin ring motif measures 1 x ¾ in. (2.5 x 2 cm.).

NOTE
Quantities given are enough for 1 runner, 4 napkins, and 4 napkin rings.

YOU WILL NEED
For the embroidery
- 41½ in. (105 cm.) E3270, 28-count white Brittney evenweave
- Tapestry needle, size 26
- Embroidery hoop
- Scissors
- Contrasting basting thread
- DMC stranded cottons as listed

To make up the projects
- Sewing machine
- Pins
- White sewing thread
- Tape measure
- Acrylic napkin rings

Color		Shade	No. of skeins
■	red	321	3

▷ Chart A

◁ Chart B

Symbol	Colorh	Shade
☒	red	321

TABLE RUNNER

1 Cut a length of fabric 55 x 18 in. (140 x 45 cm.) and hem by folding over ½ in. (1 cm.), then another 1 in. (1.5 cm.). Machine stitch in place.

2 Fold the completed table runner in half lengthwise and mark the central line with basting.

3 Stitch two lines of basting 3 in. (8 cm.) in from either end and two more at equally spaced distances, about 14 in. (35 cm.) apart, so that you will have four evenly spaced lines along the table runner when complete. This will mark the center of each row of motifs.

4 Using two strands of cotton in the needle and starting from the center out, stitch four rows of three motifs across the runner (chart A).

5 When you have completed all the stitching, remove the basting and gently press with a cool iron on the reverse of the cloth.

Below: This chic table runner has a geometric design of hearts.

◁ overlap pattern from this point

NAPKIN

1 Hem a 12 in. (30 cm.) square of fabric in the same way as for the table runner.

2 In one corner, baste two short lines about 2¼ in. (6 cm.) in from the edges. Use where they cross as the center mark.

3 Using two strands of floss, stitch the motif (chart B).

4 Remove the basting and gently press on the reverse side with a cool iron.

NAPKIN RING

1 Cut a small piece of fabric 6 x 3¼ in. (15 x 8 cm.).

2 Stitch a single heart shape from chart A in the center, using two strands of floss.

3 When you have completed the stitching, back with Vilene and make up the napkin ring using the supplier's directions.

TIP

If red is not the right color for your dining room, simply pick up a stranded cotton shade card and choose the one that will set off your table best. There are hundreds of shades to choose from—you might even want to try a variegated or metalic thread.

Right: A napkin and napkin ring complete the set.

Turkish bathroom

Spice up your bathroom with these enchanting floral motifs. Inspired by patterns found on Turkish textiles and ceramics, they will add a touch of eastern promise to your bathing. Cool blues are perfect for a bathroom and when stitched onto crisp, white linen, look fresh and modern.

SKILL LEVEL: 2

MEASUREMENTS

Worked on 32-count linen with each cross stitch worked over two fabric threads, the soap bag motif measures 4 x 3½ in. (10 x 8.5 cm.). The towel motif (which is repeated along the width of the towel) measures 5½ x 1½ in. (14.5 x 3 cm.).

YOU WILL NEED

For the embroidery
- 17 x 17 in. (43 x 43 cm.) 32-count white Belfast linen
- Guest towel with Aida panel
- Tapesty needle, size 26
- Embroidery hoop
- Scissors
- Contrasting basting thread
- DMC stranded cottons as listed

To make up the projects
- Basic sewing kit
- Sewing machine
- White sewing thread
- 3 ft. (1 m.) cord

Color		Shade	No. of skeins
■	dark blue	796	1
■	royal blue	798	1
■	baby blue	809	1
□	palest aqua	747	1
■	aqua	964	1

Symbol	Color	Shade
■	dark blue	796
☒	royal blue	798
⊟	baby blue	809
⊙	palest aqua	747
▲	aqua	964

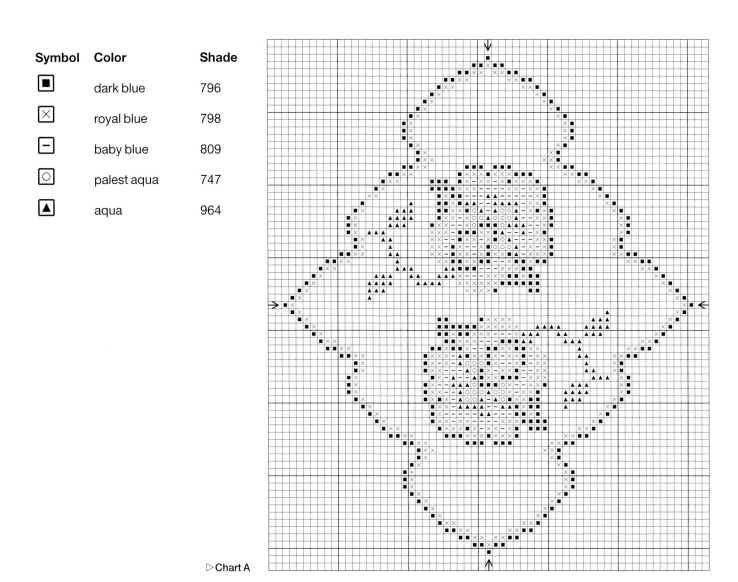

▷Chart A

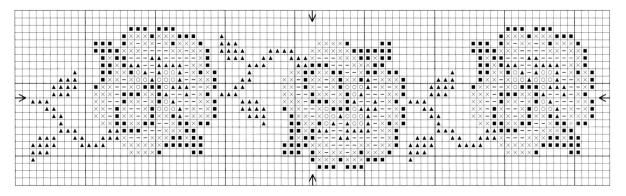

△ Chart B

SOAP BAG

1 Fold the linen in half and mark the crease with a line of basting. With the fabric laid out so the line sits vertically, measure 4½ in. (12 cm.) up from the bottom and stitch another line of basting horizontally across the first. Where the lines cross, marks the design center.

2 Using two strands of floss, begin stitching from the center out (chart A).

3 When you have completed the stitching, remove the basting and gently press on the reverse with a cool iron.

4 With the fabric face down, fold 4 in. (10 cm.) over from the top. Then, using white thread, machine stitch two parallel lines across the linen, 1 in. (3 cm.) apart and 2¼ in. (6 cm.) from the top. This will form the channel through which to thread the cord.

5 Fold the fabric horizontally, design facing inward. Taking a ½ in. (1.5 cm.) seam allowance, machine stitch down the edge, remembering to leave a gap between the parallel rows of stitching. Press open the seam and zigzag or oversew the edges to prevent fraying.

6 With this seam directly opposite the stitching and the design placed centrally on the front, take a ½ in. (1.5 cm.) seam allowance and machine stitch the bottom of the bag. Zigzag or oversew the edges to prevent fraying.

7 Turn the bag right side out and press. Then thread the cord through the channel.

Right: This blue design is inspired by Turkish tiles and ceramics.

Above: This drawstring bag is perfect for soap or cotton.

GUEST TOWEL

1 Fold the towel in half and stitch a line of basting across the Aida panel, marking the vertical center. Using a tape measure, find the horizontal center and mark with basting.

2 Using two strands of floss, begin stitching from the center out (chart B), repeating the design along the band and finishing at either end with a complete motif.

3 Remove the basting and with a cool iron, gently press on the reverse.

TIP

Do ensure all the thread ends are very firmly secured; otherwise, they may work loose when the towel is washed or used.

DMC chart

Shade no.	Column no.	Shade no.	Column no.	Shade no.	Column no.	Shade no.	Column no.	Shade no.	Column no.	Shade no.	Column no.	Shade no.	Column no.
B5200	17	334	6	598	7	783	12	922	14	3072	17	3805	4
Blanc	17	335	2	600	4	791	5	924	8	3078	13	3806	4
Ecru	17	336	6	601	4	792	5	926	8	3325	6	3807	5
48	19	340	5	602	4	793	5	927	8	3326	2	3808	7
51	20	341	5	603	4	794	5	928	8	3328	1	3809	7
52	19	347	1	604	4	796	5	930	6	3340	13	3810	7
53	20	349	1	605	4	797	5	931	6	3341	13	3811	7
57	19	350	1	606	13	798	5	932	6	3345	9	3812	7
61	20	351	1	608	13	799	5	934	10	3346	9	3813	8
62	19	352	1	610	12	800	5	935	10	3347	9	3814	8
67	19	353	1	611	12	801	16	936	10	3348	9	3815	8
69	20	355	15	612	12	806	7	937	10	3350	2	3816	8
75	19	356	15	613	12	807	7	938	16	3354	2	3817	8
90	20	367	9	632	15	809	5	939	6	3362	11	3818	9
91	19	368	9	640	17	813	5	943	8	3363	11	3819	11
92	20	369	9	642	17	814	1	945	14	3364	11	3820	12
93	19	370	11	644	17	815	1	946	13	3371	16	3821	12
94	20	371	11	645	17	816	1	947	13	3607	4	3822	12
95	19	372	11	646	17	817	1	948	15	3608	4	3823	13
99	19	400	14	647	17	818	2	950	15	3609	4	3824	13
101	20	402	14	648	17	819	2	951	14	3685	3	3825	14
102	19	407	15	666	1	820	5	954	9	3687	3	3826	14
103	19	413	18	676	12	822	17	955	9	3688	3	3827	14
104	20	414	18	677	12	823	6	956	2	3689	3	3828	12
105	20	415	18	680	12	824	5	957	2	3705	1	3829	12
106	20	420	12	699	10	825	5	958	7	3706	1	3830	15
107	19	422	12	700	10	826	5	959	7	3708	1	3831	2
108	20	433	16	701	10	827	5	961	2	3712	1	3832	2
111	20	434	16	702	10	828	5	962	2	3713	1	3833	2
112	19	435	16	703	10	829	11	963	2	3716	2	3834	3
113	19	436	16	704	10	830	11	964	7	3721	3	3835	3
114	20	437	16	712	16	831	11	966	9	3722	3	3836	3
115	19	444	13	718	4	832	11	970	13	3726	3	3837	4
116	19	445	13	720	14	833	11	971	13	3727	3	3838	5
121	19	451	15	721	14	834	11	972	13	3731	2	3839	5
122	20	452	15	722	14	838	16	973	13	3733	2	3840	5
123	20	453	15	725	13	839	16	975	14	3740	3	3841	6
124	19	469	10	726	13	840	16	976	14	3743	3	3842	7
125	20	470	10	727	13	841	16	977	14	3746	5	3843	6
126	19	471	10	729	12	842	16	986	9	3747	5	3844	6
208	4	472	10	730	11	844	17	987	9	3750	6	3845	6
209	4	498	1	731	11	869	12	988	9	3752	6	3846	6
210	4	500	8	732	11	890	9	989	9	3753	6	3847	7
211	4	501	8	733	11	891	2	991	8	3755	6	3848	7
221	3	502	8	734	11	892	2	992	8	3756	6	3849	7
223	3	503	8	738	16	893	2	993	8	3760	7	3850	8
224	3	504	8	739	16	894	2	995	6	3761	7	3851	8
225	3	517	7	740	13	895	9	996	6	3765	7	3852	12
300	14	518	7	741	13	898	16	3011	11	3766	7	3853	14
301	14	519	7	742	13	899	2	3012	11	3768	8	3854	14
304	1	520	10	743	13	900	13	3013	11	3770	14	3855	14
307	13	522	10	744	13	902	3	3021	17	3772	15	3856	14
309	2	523	10	745	13	904	10	3022	17	3773	15	3857	15
310	18	524	10	746	12	905	10	3023	17	3774	15	3858	15
311	6	535	17	747	7	906	10	3024	17	3776	14	3859	15
312	6	543	16	754	15	907	10	3031	16	3777	15	3860	15
315	3	550	4	758	15	909	9	3032	17	3778	15	3861	15
316	3	552	4	760	1	910	9	3033	17	3779	15	3862	16
317	18	553	4	761	1	911	9	3041	3	3781	16	3863	16
318	18	554	4	762	18	912	9	3042	3	3782	17	3864	16
319	9	561	8	772	9	913	9	3045	12	3787	17	3865	17
320	9	562	8	775	6	915	4	3046	12	3790	16	3866	17
321	1	563	8	776	2	917	4	3047	12	3799	18		
322	6	564	8	778	3	918	14	3051	10	3801	1		
326	2	580	11	780	12	919	14	3052	10	3802	3		
327	4	581	11	781	12	920	14	3053	10	3803	3		
333	5	597	7	782	12	921	14	3064	15	3804	4		

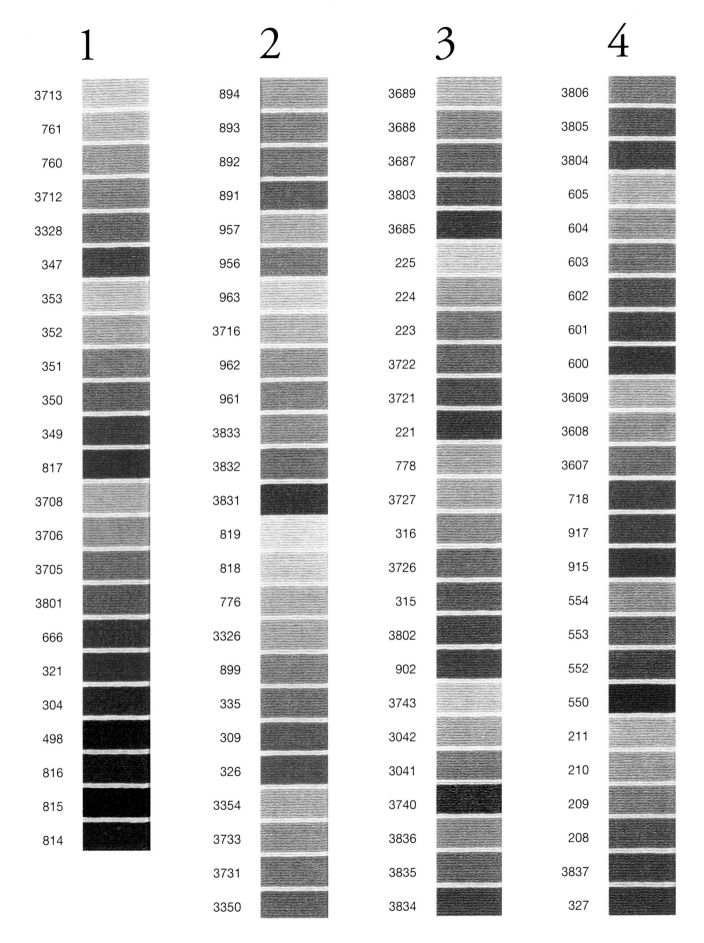

1

3713
761
760
3712
3328
347
353
352
351
350
349
817
3708
3706
3705
3801
666
321
304
498
816
815
814

2

894
893
892
891
957
956
963
3716
962
961
3833
3832
3831
819
818
776
3326
899
335
309
326
3354
3733
3731
3350

3

3689
3688
3687
3803
3685
225
224
223
3722
3721
221
778
3727
316
3726
315
3802
902
3743
3042
3041
3740
3836
3835
3834

4

3806
3805
3804
605
604
603
602
601
600
3609
3608
3607
718
917
915
554
553
552
550
211
210
209
208
3837
327

Exclusive numbering system of DMC © 2002

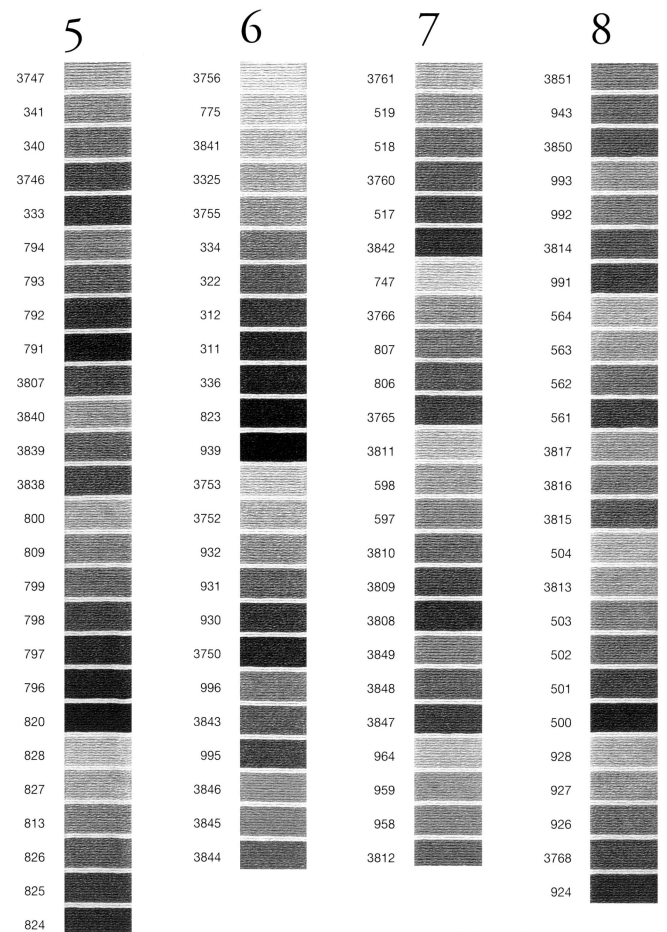

5

3747	
341	
340	
3746	
333	
794	
793	
792	
791	
3807	
3840	
3839	
3838	
800	
809	
799	
798	
797	
796	
820	
828	
827	
813	
826	
825	
824	

6

3756	
775	
3841	
3325	
3755	
334	
322	
312	
311	
336	
823	
939	
3753	
3752	
932	
931	
930	
3750	
996	
3843	
995	
3846	
3845	
3844	

7

3761	
519	
518	
3760	
517	
3842	
747	
3766	
807	
806	
3765	
3811	
598	
597	
3810	
3809	
3808	
3849	
3848	
3847	
964	
959	
958	
3812	

8

3851	
943	
3850	
993	
992	
3814	
991	
564	
563	
562	
561	
3817	
3816	
3815	
504	
3813	
503	
502	
501	
500	
928	
927	
926	
3768	
924	

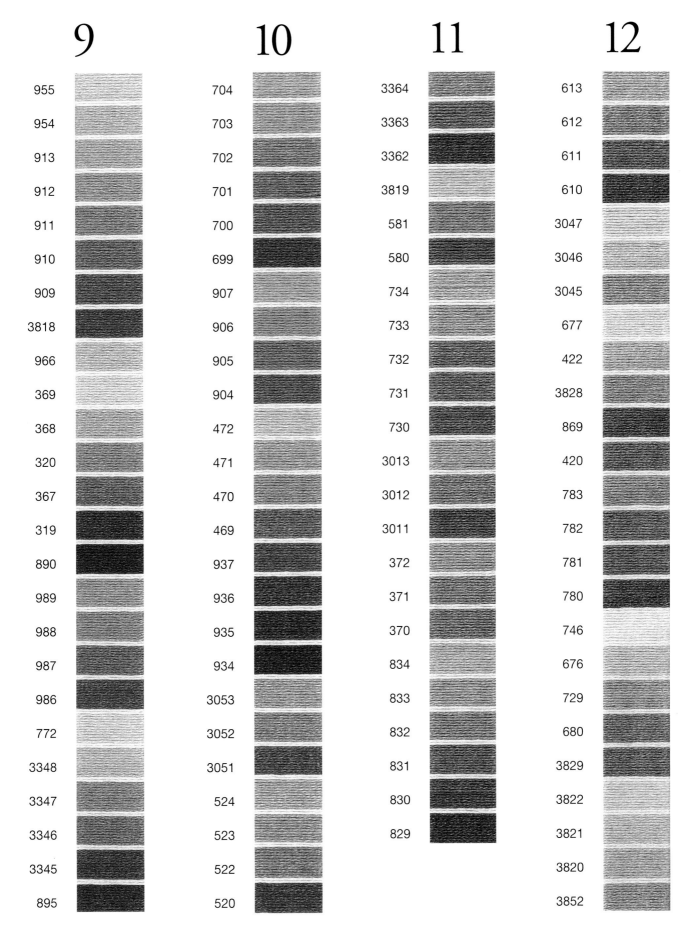

9

| 955 |
| 954 |
| 913 |
| 912 |
| 911 |
| 910 |
| 909 |
| 3818 |
| 966 |
| 369 |
| 368 |
| 320 |
| 367 |
| 319 |
| 890 |
| 989 |
| 988 |
| 987 |
| 986 |
| 772 |
| 3348 |
| 3347 |
| 3346 |
| 3345 |
| 895 |

10

| 704 |
| 703 |
| 702 |
| 701 |
| 700 |
| 699 |
| 907 |
| 906 |
| 905 |
| 904 |
| 472 |
| 471 |
| 470 |
| 469 |
| 937 |
| 936 |
| 935 |
| 934 |
| 3053 |
| 3052 |
| 3051 |
| 524 |
| 523 |
| 522 |
| 520 |

11

| 3364 |
| 3363 |
| 3362 |
| 3819 |
| 581 |
| 580 |
| 734 |
| 733 |
| 732 |
| 731 |
| 730 |
| 3013 |
| 3012 |
| 3011 |
| 372 |
| 371 |
| 370 |
| 834 |
| 833 |
| 832 |
| 831 |
| 830 |
| 829 |

12

| 613 |
| 612 |
| 611 |
| 610 |
| 3047 |
| 3046 |
| 3045 |
| 677 |
| 422 |
| 3828 |
| 869 |
| 420 |
| 783 |
| 782 |
| 781 |
| 780 |
| 746 |
| 676 |
| 729 |
| 680 |
| 3829 |
| 3822 |
| 3821 |
| 3820 |
| 3852 |

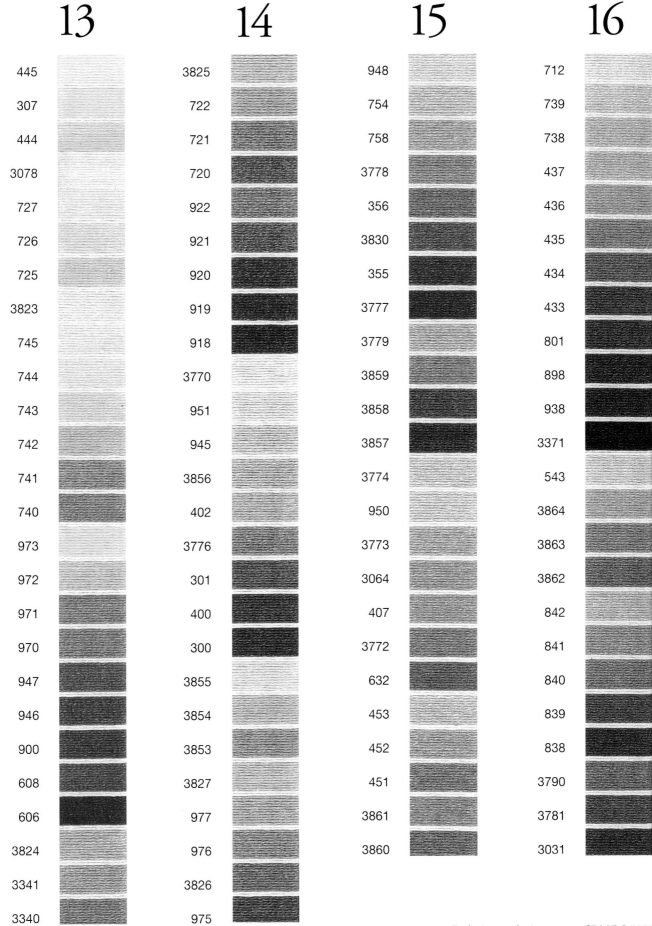

13

445
307
444
3078
727
726
725
3823
745
744
743
742
741
740
973
972
971
970
947
946
900
608
606
3824
3341
3340

14

3825
722
721
720
922
921
920
919
918
3770
951
945
3856
402
3776
301
400
300
3855
3854
3853
3827
977
976
3826
975

15

948
754
758
3778
356
3830
355
3777
3779
3859
3858
3857
3774
950
3773
3064
407
3772
632
453
452
451
3861
3860

16

712
739
738
437
436
435
434
433
801
898
938
3371
543
3864
3863
3862
842
841
840
839
838
3790
3781
3031

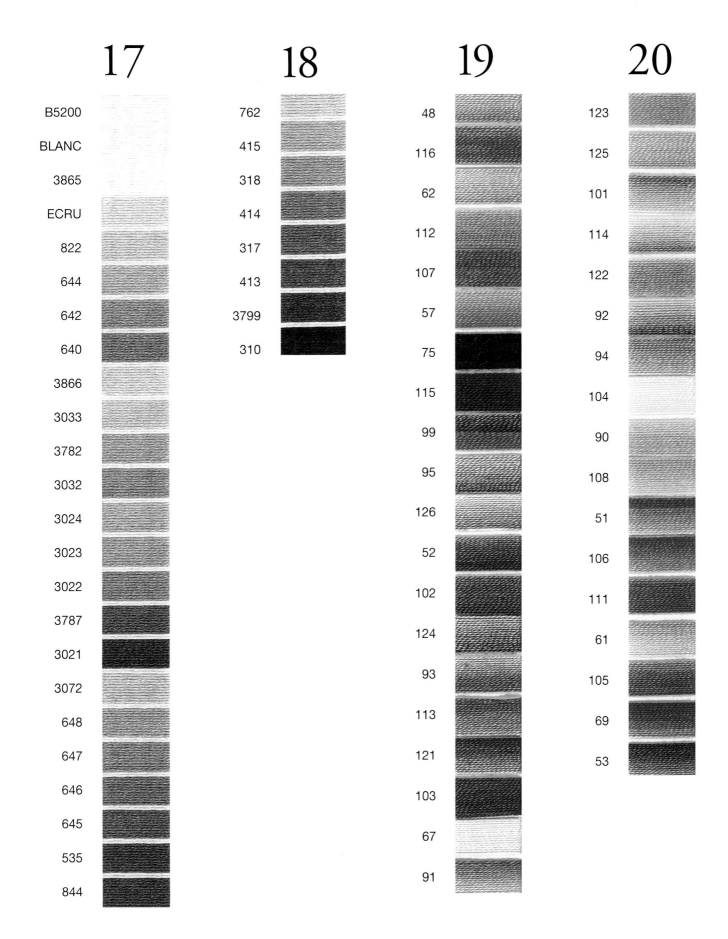

17

- B5200
- BLANC
- 3865
- ECRU
- 822
- 644
- 642
- 640
- 3866
- 3033
- 3782
- 3032
- 3024
- 3023
- 3022
- 3787
- 3021
- 3072
- 648
- 647
- 646
- 645
- 535
- 844

18

- 762
- 415
- 318
- 414
- 317
- 413
- 3799
- 310

19

- 48
- 116
- 62
- 112
- 107
- 57
- 75
- 115
- 99
- 95
- 126
- 52
- 102
- 124
- 93
- 113
- 121
- 103
- 67
- 91

20

- 123
- 125
- 101
- 114
- 122
- 92
- 94
- 104
- 90
- 108
- 51
- 106
- 111
- 61
- 105
- 69
- 53

Exclusive numbering system of DMC © 2002

Anchor conversion chart

This conversion chart should be used a guide only, because it is not always possible to provide exact substitutes.

An * indicates that the Anchor shade has been used more than once and additional care should be taken to avoid duplication within a design.

Some Anchor shades do not appear on this chart because they are unique to the Anchor range.

B5200	1	444	291	700	228	819	271	943	189	3346	267*	3808	1068		
White	2	445	28	701	227	820	134	945	881	3347	266*	3809	1066*		
Ecru	110*	451	233	702	226	822	390	946	332	3348	264	3810	1066*		
208	109	452	232	703	238	823	152*	947	330*	3350	77	3811	1060		
210	108	453	231	704	256*	824	164	948	1011	3354	74	3812	188		
211	342	469	267*	712	926	825	162*	950	4146	3362	263	3813	875*		
221	897*	470	266*	718	88	826	161*	951	1010	3363	262	3814	1074		
223	895	471	265	720	326	827	160	954	203*	3364	261	3815	877*		
224	893	472	253	721	324	828	9159	955	203*	3371	896	3816	876*		
225	1026	498	1005	722	323*	829	906	956	40*	3607	87	3817	875*		
300	352	500	683	725	305	830	277*	957	50	3608	86	3818	923*		
301	1049*	501	878	726	295*	831	277*	958	187	3609	85	3819	278		
304	19	502	877*	727	293	832	907	959	186	3685	1028	3820	306		
307	289	503	876*	729	890	833	874*	961	76*	3687	68	3821	305*		
309	42	504	206*	730	845*	834	874*	962	75*	3688	75*	3822	295*		
310	403	517	1628	731	281*	838	1088	963	872	3689	49	3823	386		
311	148	518	1039	732	281*	839	1086	964	185	3705	35*	3824	8*		
312	979	519	1038	733	280	840	1084	966	240	3706	35*	3825	323*		
315	1019*	520	862*	734	279	841	1082	970	925	3708	31	3826	1049*		
316	1017	522	860	738	361*	842	1080	971	316*	3712	1023	3827	311		
317	400	523	859	739	366	844	1041	972	298	3713	1020	3829	901*		
318	235*	524	858	740	316*	869	375	973	290	3716	25	3830	5975		
319	1044*	535	401	741	304	890	218	975	357	3721	896	48	1207		
320	215	543	933	742	303	891	35*	976	1001	3722	1027	51	1220*		
321	47	550	101*	743	302	892	33*	977	1002	3726	1018	52	1209*		
322	978	552	99	744	301	893	27	986	246	3727	1016	57	1203*		
326	598	553	98	745	300	894	26	987	244	3731	76*	61	1218*		
327	1018	554	95	746	275	895	1044*	988	243	3733	75*	62	1201*		
333	119	561	212	747	158	898	380	989	242	3740	872	67	1212		
334	977	562	210	754	1012	899	38	991	1076	3743	869	69	1218*		
335	40*	563	208	758	9575	900	333	992	1072	3746	1030	75	1206*		
336	150	564	206*	760	1022	902	897*	993	1070	3747	120	90	1217*		
340	118	580	924	761	1021	904	258	995	410	3750	1036	91	1211		
341	117	581	281*	762	234	905	257	996	433	3752	1032	92	1215*		
347	1025	597	1064	772	259	906	256*	3011	856	3753	1031	93	1210*		
349	13*	598	1062	775	128	907	255	3012	855	3755	140	94	1216		
350	11	600	59*	776	24	909	923*	3013	853	3756	1037	95	1209*		
351	10	601	63*	778	968	910	230	3021	905*	3760	162*	99	1204		
352	9	602	57	780	309	911	205	3022	8581*	3761	928	101	1213*		
353	8*	603	62*	781	308*	912	209	3023	899	3765	170	102	1209*		
355	1014	604	55	782	308*	913	204	3024	388*	3766	167	103	1210*		
356	1013*	605	1094	783	307	915	1029	3031	905*	3768	779	104	1217*		
367	216	606	334	791	178	917	89	3032	898*	3770	1009	105	1218*		
368	214	608	330*	792	941	918	341	3033	387*	3772	1007	106	1203*		
369	1043	610	889	793	176	919	340	3041	871	3773	1008	107	1203*		
370	888*	611	898*	794	175	920	1004	3042	870	3774	778	108	1220*		
371	887*	612	832	796	133	921	1003*	3045	888*	3776	1048	111	1218*		
372	887*	613	831	797	132	922	1003*	3046	887*	3777	1015	112	1201*		
400	351	632	936	798	146	924	851	3047	852	3778	1013*	113	1210*		
402	1047	640	393	799	145	926	850	3051	845*	3779	868	114	1215*		
407	914	642	392	800	144	927	849	3052	844	3781	1050	115	1206*		
413	2368	644	391	801	359	928	274	3053	843	3782	388*	121	1210*		
414	235*	645	273	806	169	930	1035	3064	883	3787	904*	122	1215*		
415	398	646	8581*	807	168	931	1034	3072	397	3790	904*	124	1210*		
420	374	647	1040	809	130	932	1033	3078	292	3799	236*	125	1213*		
422	372	648	900	813	161*	934	862*	3325	129	3801	1098	126	1209*		
433	358	666	46	814	45	935	861	3326	36	3802	1019*				
434	310	676	891	815	44	936	846	3328	1024	3803	69				
435	365	677	361*	816	43	937	268*	3340	329	3804	63*				
436	363	680	901*	817	13*	938	381	3341	328	3806	62*				
437	362	699	923*	818	23*	939	152*	3345	268*	3807	122				

Index